JOYCE FIDLER

# Evolution of a Baby Boomer

*Life Beyond Sex, Drugs and Rock 'n' Roll*

**PLATYPUS**
PUBLISHING

*I dedicate this book to all those who knew me and loved me through my wild and crazy years.*

# Contents

# Acknowledgement

Thanks to Kyrie and Rena for their forgiveness and for surviving my crappy parenting to become vibrant, productive and loving feminists.

Special love and thanks to Paul who encouraged me to write this book and for being my perfect life partner on this sober journey.

# 1

## Ch-ch-ch-ch-changes

I knew my life, our lives, would never be the same after tonight. My heart pounded as I bathed the girls for bed. This was the night I would finally tell their father my plan to start dating other men.

Rena, three, and her six-year-old sister, Kyrie, squealed and splashed in the warm tub, where a school of colorful plastic fish bobbed on the waves they created. My hand moved the Strawberry Shortcake washcloth in routine fashion over my daughters' sleek, wet backs as my thoughts raced. But any fear, any guilt that might have altered my decision before this night had been extinguished by a desire I could no longer contain.

"How are you girls doing?"

Gesualdo peered into the steamy narrow bathroom, grinning, and his innocent pleasure at witnessing our regular evening ritual unnerved my resolve to the pit of my gut. I felt sick knowing I would hurt him, but a force like a storm inside of me, a yearning as strong as my love for my children, compelled me to act or I believed I would die.

I loved him. I felt compatible with this slender, George

Harrison look-alike with the Beatle haircut. Anyone looking at my life from the outside would think I had it all.

What was that life? Gesualdo was my first lover, my college sweetheart, and my husband of ten years. We lived with our two beautiful daughters in a twenty-five-hundred square foot solar dream home we built ourselves on the acre of land that also held our first eight hundred square foot house. We owned a thriving record store/headshop, called Wonderwall, with my younger, chick-magnet brother, Gary, who rented the first house. Was I insane to risk everything I had and loved?

But inside, invisible to any observer, I was riddled with something I heard years later accurately described as a "restless, irritable and discontented" feeling.

* * *

The slender sisters giggled and screamed as I toweled them dry and helped them into their freshly laundered nightgowns. Gesualdo settled between the girls and reminded them, "We have just fifteen minutes for a story."

"Call me when you're ready to say your prayer," I said as I went downstairs to finish cleaning the kitchen. I scrubbed the counters with robotic efficiency, glad for the distraction as my anxiety skyrocketed.

I made a detour to the band rehearsal room/basement where I took a couple of hits off a joint, leaving the extinguished half sitting in the ashtray.

As I wiped the stove burners, I knew I had the most loving husband and father anyone could imagine, but I was miserable.

I'd written self-pitying bad poetry to vent my feelings:
    Dribbles on the window's edge tell the story

Of restlessness and discontent and God's glory
Though frustrations can't be met,
Know you ain't seen nothin' yet
For your cry means nothing more than a drop of rain
Try oh try to pacify with hard labor
But what's the goal, approval from your neighbor?
When your aim's the circle's end
Will it help to have a friend?
Perhaps your cry means nothing more than a drop of rain.

\* \* \*

I also whined to my social worker friend, Alice.

"You could try an open marriage," she cautioned. "The problem is, you risk meeting someone who is even more sexually compatible with you. That can ruin everything."

"I just want to experience being with someone else," I said.

Nothing else mattered to me now. I knew it was shallow and selfish, but I couldn't shake the obsession.

"We're ready, Mom," I heard Rena call.

We all knelt beside Kyrie's bed as the girls repeated the Unitarian Universalist prayer together, "We are thankful for the night, and for the pleasant morning light. For rest and food and loving care, and all that makes the world so fair. Amen."

I scooped Rena up and carried her to bed, kissed Kyrie goodnight and walked down the stairs with Gesualdo.

"Wanna go to the basement?" I asked.

"Sure. Do we have any brownies?"

My husband knew I'd be smoking if we went to the music rehearsal space below. He no longer smoked, but still enjoyed the "adult brownies" I kept on hand.

I reached into the freezer and separated a marijuana brownie from the batch in the baggie. He nuked it in the microwave for a few seconds, and munched his brownie as I grabbed two beers from the fridge and headed downstairs. As we sat in the room with carpeted walls on the scruffy gold couch facing the stage, I lit the remainder of my joint and took a deep drag.

"What's up?" Gesualdo asked as he finished his snack.

"You know I've been reading books from the library about open marriage, right?" I started.

"Yeah, you showed 'em to me."

"Well, I want to date." There. I said it. "We need to decide if you want me to move out, or if you're willing to try an open marriage. What's not negotiable is if I'm dating."

I took another hit.

He sat looking at his beer can, flipping the tab-top for a moment before he spoke. Was he going to scream at me, crazed with hurt? Were we about to have our first raging scene and scare the girls? What if he kicked me to the curb?

"It would cost a lot of money if one of us moved out. We can't really afford that. I guess if you insist on doing this, we can try an open marriage."

His voice was typically calm. He sipped at his beer as I explained.

"There's a couple in Carl Rogers' book On Human Relationships that remind me of us. They've been married ten years—- just like us—- and they're dating. Rogers calls them 'pioneers in human relationships.' We'll be pioneers, too."

Gesualdo looked straight at me. He was rational on the outside despite what turmoil he might be feeling. He said, "Maybe this is a mid-life crisis. All I can say is brace yourself for whatever I do when we're forty!"

"I make no promises about the future," I laughed. We toasted our Bud Lights, I hooked hemostats to my roach, and inhaled. Little did we know how prescient those words were.

* * *

I was ecstatic. Dating with my husband's permission was the best situation I could imagine. We could try this new lifestyle from the comfort of our nice, suburban Indianapolis house.

Just a few nights later we were at a packed local new wave club called Crazy Al's. The place held 80 people, was bright and the dance floor pulsed with happy rockers. Gesualdo was on keyboards and my brother Gary was the drummer in their band called Your Parents. I danced to the cool original set in my black t-shirt imprinted with their red slogan "Listen to Your Parents."

After their set Gesualdo was drinking, talking to fans and playing video games. He seemed perfectly pre-occupied, so I approached him.

"I'm pretty drunk and ready to leave, so Landon's gonna give me a ride home," I said. "He's staying over at Gary's tonight 'cause Gary's got a hot date."

Gesualdo didn't look up from the Pac Man machine. He turned his lips around so I could kiss him goodbye but his eyes stayed focused on the bobbing yellow icon.

"Okay, see you at home," he said.

Landon was one of Gary's drinking buddies, and a roadie for Your Parents and my band, Kicks. Landon and I had been together once before. As we walked the neighborhood to his car, I played that first encounter through my memory.

\* \* \*

The owner of Crazy Al's had booked the sensational all-female band, The Go-Go's to play his club, and he chose Kicks as the opening act. This was huge for us. The Go-Go's had the number two album in the country!

I was the lead singer for Kicks, and, because we were big fans, we played several Go-Go's tunes, so we deleted those and carefully planned our set-list. Our bass player, Shirley, and I searched the second-hand store and chose groovy new mini dresses for the show. We were determined to make the most of this opportunity of a lifetime. Maybe this would lead us to stardom!

Shirley was something of a prodigy who graduated high school at age 16. She had a pixie, oval face with a short curly bob and was a solid bass player who also played clarinet. Her wholesome looking photographer/husband Raymond promised us he'd capture the Go-Go's gig on film.

Kicks took the stage and got a loud response from the standing-room-only crowd. The first couple of songs came off without a hitch but our new guitarist had trouble keeping his guitar tuned. It was agonizing to try to build momentum with the necessary, incessant, lengthy tune-fests. By the time we played the final song, I was a mess. I thought we'd bombed big time, though the crowd remained fired up. We hurried into the basement/dressing room where The Go-Go's were waiting to go on.

"I can't believe you played one of my songs!" their bass player, Kathy Valentine, said.

I was confused. We'd taken all their songs out of our set.

"Which song was that?" I asked.

"We Don't Get Along," she said.

"We got that song from a Phil Seymour album," I blurted.

"Yeh. I wrote that song for Phil," Kathy continued. "This is the coolest thing that's happened on the tour!"

Even though she seemed thrilled, I felt mortified that we didn't know we played her song and didn't give her credit from the stage.

"How could we be so stupid?" I asked Gesualdo after the other band headed upstairs.

Someone handed me a beer when I came up to watch The Go-Go's play. I pounded it down and quickly drank another. As soon as the raucous Go-Go's set ended, and they'd played their last encore, Shirley grabbed my arm.

"Raymond has a joint. Wanna drive around the block with us?" she asked.

"Of course."

We took a quick drive and I was finally able to calm down. Weed worked for me. I'm naturally hyper, so it helped me chill out. When I got back to Crazy Al's I was ready to dance.

I took a glance around the room, but my husband was nowhere to be found. I spotted Landon standing by himself with a Budweiser in his hand. In addition to being a band roadie, he was a childhood pal of Gary's roommate Billy.

I grabbed Landon's free hand and pulled him toward the dance floor.

"C'mon," I shouted above the Blondie tune "One Way or Another" blaring in the background.

We danced to that song and the Springsteen number "You Can Look (But You Better Not Touch)" that followed. Landon was a seductive dancer and I felt like I was seeing him for the first time. He had a little boy's mostly hairless face from his native American heritage but strong biceps and smooth moves.

We danced a slow one next and I heard myself whisper to him, "You wanna go make out?"

"Ok. Where?" he answered.

"The basement."

"I'm gonna pee first. I'll meet you down there," he said.

I made my way to the basement and paced around waiting. The Go-Go's had left, so there was nobody down there and nothing to do but walk around in circles. I waited about ten minutes, but Landon never showed up. Suddenly I felt like an idiot. This was just more humiliation to add to my feelings about our mediocre gig. I headed back up the stairs not knowing what I'd say if he was still in the club.

As I came out the basement door and investigated the club I spotted my husband across the room in a booth with friends. Landon came over from the video game area and tapped me on the shoulder.

"What's up?" I said, trying to sound casual.

"Gesualdo was in the bathroom, too. He walked out with me," Landon explained. "It was kinda awkward."

Just looking at his sexy mouth I was swept with an impulse.

"Let's go," I said and turned around.

I pushed open the club's back door and he followed me into the alley. This was not an ordinary alley. It was bright with lights and had been dubbed "Action Alley."

The door was barely closed behind us when he pressed me against a wall and laid a big kiss on my lips. He was an amazing kisser, and I felt his swollen crotch push against me. The next thing I knew he'd unbuttoned the single crystal button behind my neck that was holding the top of my backless dress in place.

It folded forward to my waist, and he attacked my small breasts. I was a goner. In just another few motions my panties were at my ankles, and I held him in my hand. The silver mini-dress was flipped over us as he turned me toward the wall and thrust himself forward. I placed my hands out so I wouldn't have my face against the brick and surrendered to the glorious sensation of him inside me. It was over in just a few delicious minutes. Landon wiped himself with his underwear as I pulled mine back up.

As he re-fastened my top, I saw Keefus, a friendly, redheaded regular customer from Wonderwall standing by the door and looking our way. He smiled and walked the opposite direction out of the alley.

I went back inside first and slid around the video game wall. Landon came in a few minutes later, after smoking a cigarette. My life would never be the same.

# 2

# Commune

I finished playing that reminiscence through my mind just as we reached Landon's big burgundy Buick. Once I slid in beside him, he leaned over to kiss me.His Jack Daniels flavored kisses excited me.

It felt surreal going into my former house to sleep with a man other than my husband. Gary's was the back bedroom—-Rena's old room when she was born.

Landon and I began kissing with our clothes on but quickly tossed them to the floor. Before I knew it we were between the sheets and I felt myself submitting to this man whose lips and body made me quiver. His muscular arms were drastically different from Gesualdo's lean frame. After a long and satisfying lovemaking session I fell asleep beside him.

I hadn't been out very long when I felt Landon kissing the back of my neck. I rolled over to face him, surprised at the overture. He moved on top of me and started another round of incredible sex. I felt myself climax repeatedly as it seemed he did push-ups forever. When he finally collapsed beside me again, I had to ask, "Where have you been all my life?"

"Well, I wasn't born for a large part of it," he said.

Landon was eight years younger than I but had much more sexual experience.

"How did you get to be such a skillful lover?"

"Practice, practice, practice," was all he would say.

We decided we should both leave so we wouldn't be there when Gary got home. I tidied up the bed and slithered home across the driveway as the sun came up. Gesualdo appeared to be sound asleep as I quickly showered and crawled into bed beside him.

The next day I tried to act as normally as possible. I was in a cheerful mood as I fixed cinnamon French toast for my family, and then went down to the mudroom to begin a load of laundry. As I stood beside the washer my brother Gary appeared around the corner. He had a bundle of sheets in his arms and dumped them at my feet.

"Here. You can wash these," he barked and spun on his heels to leave.

I felt my blood pressure shoot up as I grabbed the sheets and hurled them at his back.

"Bullshit. Wash 'em yourself. If you leave them here, I'm burning them,' I said.

Gary leaned over, took the sheets, and stomped out the door. He shouted over his shoulder, "You're insane!"

Oddly enough, Gesualdo sided with me in the dispute with Gary. There had been many times over the years when my brother's sexual activities had imposed on us. When we were students in an apartment at Purdue University, Gary came for a weekend and kicked us during sex as we slept in the bed next to his. Another time he left bloody sheets behind at our house when he "boinked" a girl on her period while we were out of town.

"He's got his nerve," Gesualdo agreed.

We both knew we'd made the agreement to try an open marriage, so he didn't question me about my time with Landon. From that first overnight with my new partner, however, I was obsessed. It was the same type of pre-occupation I experienced when Gesualdo and I first got together. How was I going to spend as much time as possible with Landon and still take care of my other obligations?

\* \* \*

Our two houses were in the same neighborhood as my parents' home. Mother and Dad were my constant source of babysitting support. Dad was a retired Army Lieutenant Colonel. We were required to address our parents as "sir" and "ma'am" when we were small. Mother was a native Japanese-Hawaiian who had always been the disciplinarian in our family. As I made plans to go out, I knew I could send the kids to Mom and Dad's as usual, but I doubted it would really be enough for me.

As I pondered that idea, other situations were evolving around me. Our bass player Shirley decided she had a big crush on my husband and was spending more and more time with him.

"I told Raymond the same thing you said to Gesualdo," Shirley said. "He blew up and moved out."

Shirley and Raymond lived at her mother's house, but she'd been getting home later and later as she and Gesualdo began their love affair. It assuaged my guilt to know they liked each other but I confronted them with my fears.

"Whatever you do, just don't kick me out of the band."

Gesualdo was now playing keyboards with both Kicks and

Your Parents. Even though I'd always dreamed of becoming an actress, I was surprised to find I really enjoyed singing in a band. Regardless of how ridiculous this sounds, I was unconcerned about losing my marriage but worried I might get booted from the band.

One weekend Gesualdo bought tickets to a Springsteen concert and was taking Shirley to Cincinnati for the show. I wanted Landon to stay with me, but the girls were staying home that night.

"I think we should tell the girls what's happening," I said.

"You're probably right. I don't want them to get confused."

He and Shirley left for the concert and I'd finished serving the girls' dinner. As they left the table I called them into the living room. I wanted to get this over.

"You know how some of your friends have parents that are divorced?" I began.

"Yes," Kyrie said.

"Well people get divorced because they don't want to be together anymore. Your Daddy and I don't want to get divorced, but we do want to spend time with other people. That's why your Daddy took Shirley to see Bruce Springsteen tonight and why I went with Landon to his softball game last Sunday. I want to get to know Landon better and Daddy wants to know Shirley better. Do you understand?"

"I think so," Kyrie said.

Rena smiled and nodded her head.

"I don't want you to think this is normal. Other moms and dads who want to be with other people get divorced. Your Dad and I still love each other and want to stay married but we're going to have Shirley and Landon around, too. Is that okay with you?"

"Okay. Can we go play now?" Kyrie said.

I hugged both girls together.

"Of course. Thanks for understanding."

The girls were three and six years old. What made me think they understood or accepted what I'd just said?

# 3

# Kids and Consequences

We wanted things to stay smooth for the girls as we all adjusted to this new lifestyle. Gesualdo still read them to sleep each night. We also continued attending our church on Sundays. We were members of All Souls Unitarian Church where there was no creed, and no dogma. I was relieved to see the new arrangement seemed to be working just fine for the kids.

Landon and Shirley spent more and more time at our home, and I put all the information on the emergency contact card at school. I notified the school that it would be okay if either of the four of us picked Kyrie up from school. The assistant principal, Karen, was a woman I'd known in high school. When I saw her one day she asked me about the situation.

"How did you ever get your husband to go along with that arrangement?" Karen asked. "My husband would kill me!"

I just laughed and played it off. In my mind we were all happy and content, though my self-absorption was showing. Or maybe it was because I was perpetually high.

As the room mother for Kyrie's school Halloween party, I brought a tub with water, so the kids could bob for apples. Alas,

I forgot most first graders have no front teeth, and the kids almost drowned trying to get the apples out of the vat. Oops.

One evening Gesualdo strummed the guitar while Kyrie 'wrote' a song about our family. I transcribed the lyrics as she made up the verses and we brought the song to school when they had career day. Part of the lyrics were:

> I was born in '74, just a short time ago
> Been trying to grow up ever since
> But my parents move too slow
> Mommy, Daddy, Gesualdo and Joyce
> Laying down the law
> How can a girl just like me
> Grow up straight and tall?

Years later Kyrie told me she was humiliated to have us show up with a guitar and sing to her class.

"Why couldn't you guys have a normal job like other people?" she asked.

One mild spring Saturday morning I took the girls to the local Putt Putt course. I'd noticed that Rena was losing weight, and my friends had mentioned it, too. Her face had gotten thin, and her arms looked bony. I decided to do an experiment, so I bought each girl a large diet soda to drink as we golfed. While Kyrie's was just partially gone, Rena had consumed her entire drink. After our game I took them to the Dairy Queen across the street.

"I'm thirsty," Rena said.

"Give her that large glass with water," I told the girl with the paper DQ hat.

I parked Rena at a table with Kyrie as I waited for our soft serve ice cream cones. When I returned with our treats Rena had emptied the huge glass of water. I was secretly alarmed but thought there was nothing I could do until Monday.

Gesualdo and I were going to the symphony that night and the kids were staying with my parents. He and I still went places and did things as a couple, despite the relationships with Shirley and Landon. His family bought us season tickets to the symphony every year, so it was appropriate that we show up together.

"I just want to warn you, I think Rena may be diabetic," I said to my folks.

I told Mother about my observations. Coincidentally, she had been diagnosed with diabetes the week prior. Several people in Mother's twelve-person family were diabetics and I'd been tested for it during both pregnancies. Doctors had given me lists with all the warning signs, so I was familiar with the "excessive thirst" clue.

"Check her blood sugar if you want. I'll take her to the doctor first thing Monday morning," I said.

When we picked the kids up the next day, Mother was freaked.

"Her sugar is higher than mine!" she said.

"I'm not surprised, but the lab can't test her if she's eaten. We'll go tomorrow."

When the doctor checked Rena's fasting blood sugar levels he said, "This is a very dangerous situation. Take her to the hospital immediately. We'll keep her for a few days and get her stabilized."

At the hospital we met Dr. Gregory, a soft-spoken bespectacled endocrinologist. He gave us the plan.

"You should attend classes with a dietitian, so you'll learn how to regulate Rena's diet. We'll also teach you how to give her insulin injections."

"I don't know much about diabetes," I said. "What happens if we mess up and don't do things properly? Does diabetes ever go away?"

"No. It's a very serious disease. If Rena's not properly cared for, she could go into a coma and die. It's possible for her to live a long, productive life if you treat her condition with appropriate concern. We know there will be many complications later in life if she's not well controlled."

"We're intelligent people and teachable," I assured him.

"Tell us what to do and we'll do it," Gesualdo said.

"She needs 3 meals and 3 snacks per day. She'll also need two insulin injections every day and you'll need glucose tablets on hand for when her blood sugar drops," he said.

It felt like more than we could handle. At the time we heard this news we were also adjusting to other changes in our home. We moved Kyrie and Rena into a shared bedroom while Landon and I took Rena's room and Shirley and Gesualdo occupied the master suite. After prompting from my best friend, Sandy Tripp, I'd written Mother and Dad a five-page letter explaining our new arrangement.

"Rena might say something to your parents, so you'd better warn them first. You know what I heard her say?" Sandy told me. "I was driving Rena, Kelly and Nora home from Brownies and Nora asked Rena, 'Does your mom love Landon or Gesualdo?' Rena told her, 'Both.'"

Kelly was Sandy's youngest daughter, and Rena's best friend. Her eldest, Heidi, was Kyrie's good friend, so we six gals spent a lot of time together. Sandy knew me well and had heard my angst before I instigated all the turmoil in my home.

"Thanks for the heads up," I said.

It was also true that my parents lived just two blocks away from us and would be able to see the new collection of cars increasingly parked in our driveway every night. I smoked a joint then composed a lengthy explanation/justification of our new arrangement.

"We're like 'pioneers in human relationships'," I wrote, repeating for them the phrase I'd used to get my way. "We are trying to stay together at a time in our lives when most couples would go their separate ways."

Mother and Dad were appalled. While they said nothing to me, I knew Mom would talk with her best friend in the neighborhood, Anita Hall. Because I was a coward, I called Anita for the feedback rather than reaching out to Mom. I'd been completely straight with Mom's friend about moving Landon and Shirley into our house. I heard her light a cigarette before she related Mother's reaction.

"Yeah, your mother told me about your letter," she laughed. "She said she wishes she'd had dogs instead of children. I wouldn't worry about it. She'll be okay. It may just take some time before she calms down and gets used to the idea."

Anita was the best. She and her son Fred had the most popular house in the neighborhood. Fred was paralyzed from a diving accident while in the Navy and Anita dedicated her life to caring for him. They spoiled our children during the holidays, and on their birthdays with gifts and love.

"Come by before you go see Rena today. Fred wants to send her an orchid while she's in the hospital," Anita said.

Fred had a greenhouse full of exotic flowers attached to their family room. The doorway had been customized to accommodate his wheelchair. Gesualdo and I took the orchid and went to a hospital class to learn more about how to properly prepare a syringe of insulin.

"Think of it as a bank," Dr. Gregory said. "You must deposit air into the bottle before you withdraw the dose she needs."

The doctor released Rena from the hospital on the eve of her

19

fourth birthday.

"You can serve her an angel food cake with Cool Whip and fresh fruit," he said. "Just make sure you slice the cake into twenty pieces, so she doesn't get too much sugar. Remember, 3 meals a day and 3 snacks a day. Everything weighed, measured and on time." Damn. He said it again.

"Was Rena in a car accident or has she fallen down the stairs?" Dr. Gregory asked. "Juvenile diabetes can be the result of a trauma like that."

"Nothing more than normal childhood goofing around," I said. "The girls sometimes slide down the stairs in pillowcases, so she's banged her head a few times doing that."

Six months after Rena's diagnosis I suddenly remembered an incident that likely caused her condition.

On the date of summer solstice, we took the girls down to the center of the city for a midsummer festival. Rena finished drinking a soda and walked away from me to throw her cup in the trashcan. I turned away when I heard an old friend call my name. As I listened to my acquaintance summarize her past few years, I heard a loud POP followed by commotion and shouting.

Rena had apparently walked across an electrical cord from a popcorn vendor as it stretched across a metal grate surrounding a tree. As she stepped on the wire it exploded sending sparks and flames into the air. Thankfully, a man standing nearby saw the situation and grabbed Rena away from the flash of fire. The wire continued to burn as I snatched Rena from the man's grip and examined her to see if she was all right. Her rubber-soled tennis shoes likely saved her life. All the hair was burnt off her short legs and her long thrift-store polyester blend pants were melted as far as the knee on the inside. We hurried home with the girls, and never even considered reporting the incident to the charity sponsoring the festival.

Whenever I thought about the responsibility for Rena's health care, I became overwhelmed. I compared my situation with Anita's to pull myself out of self-pity. Anita awoke every hour to turn Fred so he wouldn't get bedsores. She'd done this for decades and I never once heard her complain. Although she never got a single night of uninterrupted sleep, Anita maintained a positive attitude and a smile on her face. What reason did I have to complain?

# 4

# What's That Smell?

We maintained the communal lifestyle for two years. Landon and Shirley now helped us at the store, in addition to being part of our family lives. They paid no rent but helped with the house, yard, and kids. Landon would occasionally talk about wanting more.

"Let's have a baby," he said.

"You know I had my tubes tied, cut and burned when Rena was two.If you wanna have babies, you need a different partner."

Shirley was apparently making some of the same noises.

"She wants me to divorce you and marry her," Gesualdo said.

"What do you want to do?"

"I told her we're staying married. That's still the plan, isn't it?"

"That's my plan."

Although we were still married, we no longer slept together. He and Shirley were monogamous, as were Landon and I. We could sometimes hear their lovemaking on the other side of the wall, but it didn't bother me. I knew Gesualdo loved me, and I wasn't threatened by his feelings for Shirley.

In the meantime, our band was still playing and changing. Our guitarist and drummer were long gone, we'd hired Gary's tall, good-looking roommate, Billy, on rhythm guitar and a five-foot tall drummer who we dubbed Little Oscar. A short, chubby woman whose stage name was Amanda Reckonwith played lead guitar. Now we had a 3-girl, 3-guy line-up and I was booking gigs around the Midwest. Our new band name was The Obvious and we played clubs in Detroit and the university towns of Champaign, Illinois and Bloomington, Indiana.

"Our tiny drummer sits backward with a huge set of drums in front of him. He sometimes does back-flips off the stool and is very entertaining. We sing Supremes and Go-Go's songs and lots of originals," I told club owners.

They often booked the group sight unseen. I could provide references from other clubs, too. We were now playing at the popular Patio, Vogue and Crazy Al's clubs in Indianapolis.

We won a "Battle of the Bands" sponsored by a recording studio, TRC. It was a prestigious studio where John Mellencamp recorded "Crumblin' Down." Our prize was eight hours of free recording at TRC.

"It's not much time, so let's record a 45," I said.

Gesualdo and I'd been writing several songs. One of our reggae-flavored tunes "Why Can't it Wait?" received a Certificate of Merit in the 1982 American Song Festival sponsored by Billboard magazine. The certificate says it's for, "Excellence in creative writing, originality, technical skill and talent in composition."

"Let's use "Why Can't it Wait?" for side A and "Ssss" as the side B track," Gesualdo said.

The lyrics of "Why Can't it Wait?" immortalized the status of our relationship.I sang the verses (which represented Gesu-

23

aldo's actual feelings) while he sang the part of the duet that expressed my sentiments. We brought Bob Liederbach in to add the emotional guitar solo. These are some of the lyrics:

When I arrive home late-I hear the phone is ringin'

Am I supposed to tolerate-all this pain you're bringin'

CHORUS:

You keep sayin' you know it all, but, baby, you don't know nothin'.

You keep kickin' me I'm already down... You think you're so bad...

You think you're so bad.

DUET:

Don't tell me now (Don't tell me now)

Talk to me later (Why can't it wait?)

Things can't be any worse (Might be too late)

They've got to get better

Why can't you see (Why can't you see?)

It's been all it can be (Is it too late)

Time is so precious (Might be too late)

Love is more than a moment to me

\*\*\*\*

Band members seemed edgy as we began the recording process. Shirley's drinking was escalating. She and Oscar laid down the rhythm (bass and drums) tracks first and left for home while we put the other instruments and vocals on tape. Shirley was home with the kids when we finally finished our day of recording. Kyrie met us at the door.

"Shirley's upstairs crying again," she said.

The pattern was starting to worry me. Shirley would often take a bottle of booze, go up to the bedroom, drink and sob.

"It's probably not good for the girls to see," I complained.

In hindsight I think Shirley was depressed because she really wanted to marry my husband and have his babies.

"He's an amazing father," she'd say when she saw Gesualdo trotting around the carpet with the girls taking turns riding on his back.

Eventually, Shirley announced that she'd joined the Army and was leaving town!

"They say I'm going to be a code breaker," she said.

She packed her bags and was gone in just a few days. Three months later I saw Shirley riding an "up" escalator in the Burlington Coat Factory at the mall. I heard the Army wouldn't give her the high security clearance required for the promised job, so she refused to get on the bus for basic training. I imagined the problem stemmed from their background check revealing that she was living with a married man and his family. She stayed away from us, though, and didn't respond when I called her name at the mall.

Things in our house got weirder with Shirley gone. Gesualdo was now alone, so he offered us the master suite, and he moved into the room Landon and I shared. Shortly after we made that change, I was in his room vacuuming one day. I noticed a funky, musty odor in the room that had never been there before.

"See if you can tell me what you smell," I asked both men and the girls.

None of us could figure out what it was. Days turned into weeks and the mystery continued. Finally, one day I was determined to find the source. I got down on my hands and knees and crawled around the floor inch by inch, sniffing the room. When I got to the closet the smell got stronger. I looked up and couldn't believe my eyes.

# 5

# Alone Together

The roof of the closet was completely black with thick mold! It reeked and looked like smudged charcoal. We reported the mess, but we'd called the builder to communicate other construction problems, without satisfaction. The tile wall of the master shower had caved in, and the wall of the guest bathroom shower was buckling.

Eventually an arbitrator resolved our dispute with the builder. Our homeowner's insurance paid for the roof and ceiling repairs and the contractor repaired the bathroom walls and tile. In my mind the rotting, crumbling new house was symbolic of the condition of our marriage.

Gesualdo's bedroom was unlivable during the re-construction. He pitched a blue tent (we'd bought for our honeymoon trip to Hawaii) in the massive side yard of our house and slept in a sleeping bag for the following weeks. I never asked him why he chose to stay outdoors, but I discussed his choice with Landon.

"He knows he can stay in the basement on the couch," Landon said.

"There's also room in the office," I said. "Maybe he's just sad about Shirley leaving and wants to be alone."

After Shirley had been gone a few months, Landon introduced Gesualdo to a childhood friend of his. Michelle was a long-legged blond who had a few dates with Gesualdo, but she lived in Louisville, Kentucky. He wrote a haunting song called "Halloween" about her. I helped him with the lyrics and chose to ignore the pain in his phrases.

There were many days when I was lonely
Losing love's not easy- never funny.
Thinking back I wonder was I dreamin'?
Looking to the future now I'm schemin'
These are tears of joy that I am crying
You opened up my heart and now I'm finding
Chorus:
Oh Halloween-Oh Halloween,
Halloween! Halloween!

I can function, I can live with sadness
Keeping it inside is only madness
Waiting for the time or special moment
Life can come and go with Halley's Comet
A face so warm, a smile that's so inviting
Eyes of turquoise, hair of golden lightning
Chorus
A voice so mild, a countenance defending
Did you think I'd see the end impending?
Chorus
Living on your own can keep you thinking
What's the way to keep your heart from sinking?
Putting trust in love can be deceiving

Autumn's in the air and you are leaving
Images of you are quickly fading
Seasons change, love's spirit still evading
Chorus

\* \* \*

After a few trips back and forth from Kentucky, we never saw Michelle again. Not surprising that single women weren't receptive to a relationship with a man who insisted up front that his marriage would stay intact. Landon confided that he heard lots of crap on the subject from his softball buddies, too.

"You're a good man," they said. "You don't have to play second string to any other man."

"I'm not second fiddle," Landon said. "Don't judge me till you've walked in my moccasins. This works for me."

As we finished the house repairs, my perspective on our life was changing. Gesualdo seemed morose much of the time. He sat at the Steinway and played for hours. I felt guilty and uncomfortable with my ongoing love affair under our roof. At last, I realized it was unfair to continue the bizarre arrangement.

\* \* \*

The 1983 economy was in a deep recession and the record industry was hurting. At Wonderwall we lost money on paper for years, so I tried to find new ways to generate business. I suggested getting into videotapes. Even though he was a minor partner in our store, we needed Gary's agreement to go forward with a radical change. He still seemed pissed at me for the Landon relationship and shot down all my ideas.

"Video isn't going to be any big deal," Gary said.

Just a few months later MTV was on the air, video had skyrocketed, and Gary admitted his shortsightedness. A video store opened in our neighborhood, and we were too late to be the chosen retailer for that product.

I read about a machine called the Xpress printer that could make an ink transfer from any picture or written document. The transfer could be applied to any paper, fabric, or metal object with a heat press (which we already owned). Store clerks would be able to make t-shirts, hats, menus, trophies, or any number of items. I invited the manufacturer to bring the machine to our 1500 square foot, fluorescent lit store for a demonstration and tried to persuade our employees to help me sell merchandise at county fairs, state fairs or our store. Gary immediately nixed the idea.

"Not interested," Dan-o said. Dan-O was a burly, curly haired, mellow guy who I expected would jump at the idea to bring us his hockey team's t-shirt business.

Dirt was my lanky lifelong pal and high school classmate who was married to a firecracker, Bridgette—-the drummer of the first band I'd joined, Lip Service.

"I really don t wanna work at fairs," Dirt shrugged.

Only our newest employee, Harlow, was willing to help. He wore glasses, sported a blonde Beatle 'do and was generally more agreeable, but his offer of support was insufficient. The machine cost $7,000 so I felt uncomfortable making the commitment if the staff refused to get on board with my idea. Their resistance irritated me.

"Fuck 'em," I told Gesualdo. "Let's just close the store and the dumbasses can go look for a job someplace else."

We reached the end of our leasehold in May of 1983 and decided to close Wonderwall forever. It was traumatic for Gesualdo to face the end of his dream store. He became more and more distressed, as the date grew closer. He vented his anxiety in an upbeat song about the advice we received from an accountant who told us to, "Take care of your family. Don't pay any more bills. Whatever funds you raise from the final days of operation should go to pay notes of investment you never collected."

The dance song was called "Corporate Punishment," and we started the recording with a martial drumbeat.

These days I'm not so very kind

Don't hesitate to speak my mind

But that's all right.

Business is business they all say

Take all you can and get away

Out of sight

Don't be afraid, don't be ashamed.

Action and words are not the same;

Day and night.

Chorus:

What will I be with no conscience to see

What is right in my heart?

You look me in the eye again

Tell me to lie to a friend

Is that okay?

It's not as easy as you say

Ten years of true integrity

Down the drain.

Friendship and camaraderie

Mean more than security;
Can I explain?
Chorus
Bridge
When I was just a child
Mother said to me
Always tell the truth now
Make sure you never lie.
Now that I'm older
I see the rules are changing
Am I to blame for not playing a game
I can't win?
One day when I am looking back
Want to be proud of the fact...
My debts were paid
There may not be another chance
To face such unfair circumstance
Was I betrayed?
This is the end, I understand,
I will not break what can never mend;
That's insane

\* \* \*

We couldn't fathom sticking it to people with whom we'd established years of trust and friendship. Gesualdo and I would close our doors with every vendor and tax liability paid, even if it meant walking away from the thousands of dollars owed to us by the business.

"I don't think I can handle selling off the final merchandise and shutting the doors forever," he said. "Phat wants to take a trip to L.A. and I'd like to go with him."

# 6

## Let Me Stand Next to Your Fire

Phat was one of Gesualdo's fraternity brothers from the Pike house at Purdue. He was a bearded and ginger haired pharmacist/sax player working in Indy who was single, and ready for a male bonding adventure.

"Understandable," I said. "We can handle all the final details. Go enjoy yourself."

I was relieved Gesualdo was leaving. Even though I shared his uncertainty about the future it was too painful watching him struggle with our decision.

"I wanna start my own store," Dirt announced as we entered the last month of business.

"Be my guest," I said. "We'll just send the Wonderwall customers to you."

It was very emotional seeing customers for the last time. Kyrie was now nine years old. She sat behind the cash register on a tall stool and rang up customers as they herded past with stacks of bargains.

"I remember when she used to be here in a bassinet," several folks commented.

"You freaked me out when you held her with one arm so she could nurse, while you rang up my sale with your other hand," others reminded me.

There were plenty of hugs and tears as I said good-bye to the people who'd become cherished acquaintances over our decade-long relationship.

Once the empty record racks and display cases were carted over to Dirt's new location, we disassembled the barn-wood walls of the store and paneled the laundry room of our house with them. In that way we kept some of the Wonderwall "vibe" alive.

Gary went to work at Scott's One Stop as a record wholesaler. Dan-o and Harlow also took jobs in Scott's warehouse.When he returned from L.A. Gesualdo started working at T&L, his family's sheet metal business, and I went back to school.

I enrolled at Butler University to complete a master's degree in radio and television. I chose a minor in guidance and counseling so I could explore the psychological implications of my wacky lifestyle. As a student I was entitled to free counseling services.

"Will you go with me to therapy?" I asked both Gesualdo and Landon.

"No way," Landon said. "That shit is stupid."

"Sure," my husband said. "It's worth a try."

We had the girls assessed first. The therapist said Kyrie showed signs of "internalizing her affect."I thought that meant she was just fine. Rena's test results were more direct and disturbing, "...she may be having some difficulty with anxiety and emotional stability, some feeling of inadequacy and insecurity in dealing with her environment." Then the assessment gave me an "out" when it said, "...possibly related to her diabetes or perhaps to other aspects of her life." The therapist suggested

Rena be given, "structured time alone with a significant adult (the same adult each week, possibly her mother) ...in order to create a stable relationship in which Rena will feel free to talk about her concerns." We didn't consider the suggestion too alarming since Rena really did speak openly and freely with her father, Landon and me.

"I love our kids, but I definitely don't want any more," Gesualdo said after hearing the evaluations. "I never want to argue about that issue again."

The painful ending of his relationship with Shirley had left its mark. With that, he got a vasectomy.

The therapy sessions for Gesualdo and me were twisted.

"Write your definition of marriage," the grad-student-therapist told us at our first session.

Naturally I wrote my definition to allow for the lifestyle I'd designed. My husband wrote a conventional description.

"How do these look to you?" the therapist asked him.

"Exactly the same," he answered.

I was confused. Was he really that deluded? I hoped the therapy sessions would help me decide what I should do.

After a few counseling appointments, Landon and I talked.

"If I'm going to be married to Gesualdo, I should be with him. If you and I are going to be together I should let him be free to find another partner."

"Are you telling me to date?" Landon asked.

"Do whatever you need to do. Maybe look for someone who wants to have kids. I'm gonna try to put this marriage back together, so you need to move out."

Gesualdo seemed happy with my decision. I bought us a new waterbed for Valentine's Day, 1984 and we started our reunion on all new bedding. It felt like a fresh start. There was only one problem.

Landon moved with a softball teammate to an apartment half a mile down the street from our house. He started work later than my husband, so he'd stop by to see me on his way past—-every day. He went on a few dates with other women, but "I'm not interested in anyone else. Let's see how things go with us," he said.

Also, my resistance lasted only a few days before we resumed our love affair. The only thing different was that I no longer slept overnight with Landon.

Gesualdo and I continued going to therapy, but I was now cheating on him.

"Make yourself available this weekend. I've given your husband an assignment," the therapist said. But he didn't ask to talk.

Another odd thing happened almost immediately. After working at T&L in the sheet metal shop Gesualdo came home one night and accidentally punctured the waterbed with a sliver of stainless steel that was stuck to his body. Our reconciliation seemed doomed. We patched the mattress, but it continued leaking and we often woke with a cold, wet, saggy bed beneath our bodies.

Things hobbled along like this for six months before Landon left for an annual softball trip to Canada. I was consumed and miserable while he was gone. His first night back in town I hurried over to his place. After a brief lovemaking session, I called home.

"I want to stay here tonight," I said. There was a pause.

"Go ahead if that's what you want to do, but I don't want Landon staying here again," Gesualdo declared.

Now we began a whole new dance. I went back and forth

between staying at home and staying at Landon's for the next eight months. The mornings when I stayed at Landon's I had to race home before Gesualdo left so I could get the girls ready for school. It was difficult and chaotic for me to cover all my obligations. Those months were the worst for me. In fact, I now had a bed in the office, so I slept alone when I was at home. We abandoned the pretense of renewed commitment.

Another new dynamic had developed. Gary no longer lived in our little house across the driveway. He moved after Landon and I became involved to show his disapproval of our situation. Gesualdo and I sold the house to a young couple, Albert and Rosemary and their little boy. She was consumed with my husband, and he was slowly responding to the attention. Rosemary and her husband had already been divorced once and remarried, but their marriage was not going well. She seemed enamored of our polyamorous arrangement and spent more and more time visiting our house and watching band rehearsals, flirting openly with Gesualdo.

In the meantime, the band had shifted again. The Obvious was long gone and we spent several months getting over the last, painful breakup of band personnel. We learned about Little Oscar's apparent slide into hardcore drug addiction when we found a syringe (different from Rena's) on our steps while loading out of the basement for a final gig.

One day the phone rang and Gesualdo answered it.

"I've seen every band you and Joyce have been in, and I love your original songs," the guy on the phone said. "I play rhythm guitar and we have a rhythm section and a lead guitarist. Let's see if we can put something together."

"Give me your information," Gesualdo said."Joyce and I will talk it over and get back to you."

"What do you think?" he asked me.

"I don't want to get into the same situation we had before," I said."Did you ask him if they're drug addicts?"

"Actually, he brought it up. His name is Jack Gummer and he said they don't want any cokeheads in their band. He said something about having trouble with cocaine in the past. He said they smoke pot and drink, but that's it."

"I guess it can't hurt to check 'em out," I said.

Jack, Kenny, Mike and Welch were a solid band. None of them wrote originals, but they were enthusiastic about our songs. Jack wore glasses, was super skinny with curly dark hair and a Keith Richards fanatic who played bluesy, soulful guitar. Kenny played rowdy lead guitar and was a big stoner (a huge attraction to me). He was a single dad whose son came to most of the rehearsals. Mike was a powerful, wide-eyed African American drummer who'd been in bands with Kenny since high school. Welch had a day-job selling technical equipment to hospitals. He was a small man with a quiet, wise voice and was a comfortable bass player. We liked these guys. It seemed odd to now be the only female in the band, but I got comfortable quickly.

Again, we changed the name of the band, and became Abstractions. We released our 45rpm record under that name and left the old players' names off the sleeve. The cover featured a cellular looking painting by my brother-in-law, Jan Martin.

"You should go to New York and try to find us a manager," Gesualdo said.

I wrote my high school friend Jane Pauley who was co-hosting The Today Show in the early years of her lifelong broadcasting career. She and I were on the high school speech team together and we sang in the patriotic Up With People group, Sing Out '66.

My neighbor, Sandy, went with me on the trip, and Jane invited us up to a taping of The Today Show in Rockefeller Plaza.

We were two Midwest moms who were thrilled to be on the pass list when we arrived at the famous office building. The moment the elevator doors closed Sandy turned to me and said, "I'm impressed!"

"How may I help?" Jane asked after introducing us to the rest of The Today show cast. Despite her impressive success, Jane was still the down-to-earth fresh-faced woman I'd known in school.

"Do you know any music managers?"

"My husband's college roommate was Ken Kragen. Maybe I can put you together with him," Jane said.

"That would be fantastic. He's on my list of people to contact," I said.

Jane's offer was the strongest lead we gained during that trip. A meeting with an Atlantic records A&R (artist and repertoire) executive left me frustrated.

"What? No video?" was his response to the record I handed him.

Ken Kragen was the manager for Lionel Ritchie, Kim Carnes and many other stars. He was involved in organizing the anti-hunger project "Hands Across America." When Kragen came to Indianapolis for planning that event Gesualdo and I were invited to meet him at a breakfast. My only chance to pitch him was when I shook his hand on the way out the door.

"Yes, we are looking for new artists to represent," he said. He pulled out a card and wrote some letters on it." Put this code on your package when you submit it to my office. That's how they know it's not unsolicited material."

I was hopeful and encouraged by Kragen's response. Despite

our best efforts, my package eventually came back sealed exactly as I sent it. Nobody had opened it or listened to our record. The enclosed note was generic.

"While it is true we are looking to book new talent, we are seeking established artists wishing to change representation. Thank you for your interest." An assistant signed the note.

The next day I read in Billboard magazine that Kragen had signed the Bee Gees to his talent roster.

We had been members of Abstractions for a few months when Jack showed up at rehearsal with a huge revelation.

"Did you see my brother, Don, on the Academy Awards last night?"

"I didn't notice. What was he doing at the Academy Awards?" I asked.

"His wife was winning best actress," Jack beamed.

"Your brother is married to Meryl Streep?" I screamed.

Streep had picked up the Oscar for her work in Sophie's Choice. That remote connection with greatness through our guitarist helped to keep us fired up about future possibilities.

On a later visit to Indy, Don came with Jack to hear our band rehearse in the basement. Still later, we were scheduled to play a gig when the phone rang. It was Jack.

"Hey, you can't tell anyone, due to security, but Don and Meryl are coming to the gig tonight."

Indeed, a few hours later we were on stage at The Humming-bird with them in the audience! I'm not saying it was a slow news year, but their appearance at our show was listed in The Indianapolis Star as one of the cool things that happened in 1984.

* * *

When I returned from New York, Abstractions went back into TRC studios and, over the course of the next year, we recorded an EP—- an extended play record with six songs on it. We included all original songs except for one.

Jack convinced us that we should put our reggae-tinged version of the Rolling Stones song "The Last Time" on the record. I attained the rights, and we laid it down. Once again, the recording process separated the "men from the boys." By the time the lengthy project was finished, we had more changes in our line-up. Welch, Kenny and Mike, (the three players who came with Jack), were all out. We no longer used a lead guitarist. Rather, we selected a kick-ass bass player, Eddy Humphrey and his friend Pat Schaefer who was a sexy, talented female saxophone player. Eddy, a large, clove-cigarette-smoking guy also brought a tiny, balding, but energetic drummer, Kevin Kouts.

"We'll make a video of the song DJ's like best," Gesualdo and I told the band. We were paying for all the recording and production expenses with proceeds from money he inherited when his beloved, elegant Aunt Becky died.

I submitted the completed EP called *Check it Out* to record pools around the country. DJ's subscribed to these pools as a way to get free promo records to play in clubs. Their obligation was to send feedback to the record label. The data was overwhelming. A song I wrote named "Wah Wah" was the clear favorite so we began planning the video project after DJs reported people heading to the dance floor when it played.

I wrote the song vocally in the shower in ten minutes, and sang it to our then-guitarist Amanda Reckonwith who added intro. music. The song was my attempt at writing a song with a nonsense lyric, but it was obviously an homage to my relationship with Landon and his job as our roadie. These are the words:

Hello,Po-twah.
You make me dance, ooh baby-wah.
You move so good-wah
When we romance ooh baby-wah
Chorus:
You know I love you wah, wah, wah.
You my Po-twah
Why did you go wah?
When all the boys left, ooh baby-wah
I thought you'd wait-wah
Till I could get home ooh baby-wah
Chorus
Why'd you think that I would understand
You had a love affair with a big blue van
When will I learn to relate
To my mechanical man and my new-found fate?

\* \* \*

Landon, Gesualdo and I sat talking at the dining room table after a Sunday dinner in May of 1985 when the carved tin Mexican chandelier above our heads suddenly went dark. The rest of the house lights remained lit.

"That's weird," Gesualdo said.

He looked out the window toward Sandy's house where the

girls were playing with Heidi and Kelly.

"Sandy's lights are on," he said.

"I just called the girls home," I said. "I'll go make sure the yard light is on for them."

I went to the French doors and looked right. The neighbors' house lights were glowing through their windows.

As I looked left for the yard light I gasped.

"The light is out, and the house is on fire!" I shouted.

# 7

# The Mansion

Gesualdo and Landon ran out the French doors and looked at the corner of the house where smoke was trailing into the inky sky.

"I'll grab the hose," I said.

"Let me go look in the attic," Landon said, as he turned to run back inside and up the stairs.

"I'll get the ladder," shouted Gesualdo.

After I pulled the hose in place, I stood ready to hold the ladder as Gesualdo climbed with the hose. Landon came down from the attic in a panic.

"The rafters are on fire. It's not safe for us to try hosing this down ourselves. You have to call the fire department."

Kyrie and Rena suddenly ran wild-eyed up to the house. As Gesualdo hurried past to call for help they saw Landon and me looking up at the rising smoke.

"Is our house burning down?" Kyrie cried.

"It's on fire so we have to get outta here. Go up to your room and choose one favorite toy then meet us back out in the front yard," I said as we all ran inside.

After he hung up the phone, Gesualdo gathered Rena's diabetes supplies, we filled a grocery bag with important papers, jewelry, and photo albums, and were out the front double doors in minutes. Landon moved our cars away from the garage and joined the kids and us where we waited in the darkness for the sound of approaching sirens.

As we stood beside the house our yard began to fill with people. It took just six minutes for the firemen and trucks to arrive and begin their work. Apparently, the fire could be seen for miles because of the height of our solar home. One curious lady came up to me as the girls held their Aunt Pam-made Cabbage Patch dolls and my legs. We watched the flames shooting from the roof.

"Is this your house?" she asked.

"That's right."

"Why aren't you hysterical? I'd be losing it if this was my house," she said.

"I spent yesterday in a stress management class," I told her. "The house and everything in it are just 'stuff.' My family is out of the house and everybody's safe. We can always buy more 'stuff.' The house will burn whether I'm hysterical or not. The kids need me to stay calm."

I couldn't believe these words were coming out of my mouth, but I knew we were doing everything we could. Fire hoses were shooting tons of water onto the roof, and we were watching from a safe distance.

We were now in Rosemary's living room trying to figure out who we should call to report our loss when a man knocked at the door.

"I'm Ken Gregory and I fix fires," he said. There stood a short round man with a kind face and an easy manner. "Do you have a basement?"

"Yes, we do," Gesualdo said.

"When the firemen leave it will be important to get your electricity re-connected so you don't have a flood to go with your fire. You need your sump pump working," he said.

"I would've never thought of that," I said.

"We need to call our insurance company and see what they say," Gesualdo added.

"Absolutely," Ken said. "I'll be waiting outside."

I got the insurance adjuster on the line.

"What's the name of the guy who offered to help?" the adjuster asked after I told him about the stranger.

I looked at the card in my hand.

"Ken Gregory."

"Hire him. He's excellent. He'll save you a lot of money and grief."

Several hours later the crowd and fire department were gone. By then Ken had a crew of guys who jumped into action.

"The water on that roof is threatening your upstairs ceilings. We need to get all the furniture out of the second floor and onto the lower floors. You folks grab some clothes for the next few days, and we'll get to work," Ken said.

My neighbor Sandy's husband was out of town, as usual. He worked on the road as a bigwig for a loan company. Sandy invited us to stay on her couches while we figured out a plan. The girls stayed with Heidi and Kelly in their tidy upstairs bedrooms. Gesualdo slept on the couch in the cozy family room while Landon and I crashed in the formal living room. It was the first time Gesualdo, Landon and I stayed under the same roof since Landon had moved out. The fire represented empirical evidence that our marriage was officially toast.

\* \* \*

The insurance company said it would take several months to rebuild our house.We needed a place big enough for the band to rehearse because we had several gigs booked and the video shoot coming up. We also needed a place with a kitchen so we could keep Rena's dietary needs on schedule. As we thought about all our options one of Landon's buddies (and my favorite stoner pal) Ricky came up with an idea.

"Come check out this place next to the cemetery," Ricky said.

The house was a five thousand square foot mansion on five acres with huge Gone With the Wind-type pillars in front. It was vacant and listed for sale.

"Maybe our insurance company can negotiate for us to rent the house," I told Gesualdo. "It'll be cheaper than putting us in a motel and paying for a rehearsal hall for the band."

Incredibly, the owners agreed to $650 per month for the duration of our re-construction. Of course, we agreed that prospective buyers could continue to view their property.The fabulous old mansion had floor-to-ceiling green tile in the kitchen/ breakfast nook. There were three large bedrooms upstairs and one huge bedroom downstairs. At the back of the house was a wood-paneled family room where the band set up their equipment. Behind the house were a three-car garage with servant's quarters above, and a spacious basketball court in front. Landon and I moved into the downstairs bedroom of the mansion as the girls and their father claimed the upstairs rooms.

Meanwhile, Ken Gregory was hard at work repairing our home. He had to replace the entire solar roof. Additionally, ceilings in the master and corner bedrooms were ruined.

"What caused the fire?" Ken asked.

"We think a bird built a nest in the corner of the house where the yard light intersected with the gutter's downspout. The light must have caught the nest on fire and traveled to the rafters," Gesualdo said.

"Three years earlier we put out a fire in that same location," I said.

In the previous case Landon had knocked the bird's nest to the ground where he hosed out the fire. He climbed on a ladder and inspected the wiring that looked just fine. The light worked perfectly for another three years before the new fire broke out.

When we originally built our house, Gesualdo's family business, T&L, had built our solar collectors for only their cost. They were designed and hand crafted by his middle brother, Jan. Now we learned that T&L was too busy with other client projects to re-build our fire-ruined collectors. Cost estimates from commercial manufacturers came in at $15,000, so we decided not to replace them. We would never recoup that much in energy savings in Indiana with its halftime sunshine.

"The mortgage company insists that they get a repaired house with equal or greater value," I told Gesualdo. "Since we aren't replacing the solar panels, let's expand the living space."

The steep solar roof provided the perfect large attic area for growth.

"Can you put a stairway here?" I asked Ken Gregory, gesturing at a solid wall outside the master bedroom.

"It just might fit," he said. "The staircase will have to be pretty steep, but I think I can make it work."

We agreed to build separate living quarters. As Ken designed and built my husband's new 900 square foot upstairs room, I focused on moving forward with my master's degree and the band's projects.

* * *

I was learning more about myself through courses called "Sexuality Issues in Counseling" and "Personality and Careers." I submitted a paper called A Defense of Marijuana Use by Adults and another that detailed my personal sexual history.

One day I was jolted by a professor's observations of my life. We'd just completed a test designed to measure our homo or heterosexuality. Predictably, my score was off the chart in the hetero category. Students broke into small groups to examine each other's results.

"I'd say my score is pretty accurate," I told the four classmates in my group. "It seems about right for a person living with both her husband and boyfriend."

Just as those words came out of my mouth the professor walked up to our circle.

"You're living with whom?" he asked.

I briefly explained the arrangement again.

"Oh, I get it," he said. "You're just divorced without the piece of paper."

I felt my face turn red.

"No way," I stammered. "We have no plans to get a divorce."

"Look, Joyce," he calmly continued. "A marriage is between two people. You have three people living in your house. That is not a marriage."

With that, he left our group and moved on to the next circle of students. I was stunned. Nobody had ever busted me with such directness or clarity before. I thought about his comments until the class met the next week. After class I asked the professor (who was head of the counseling department) if he would take over the therapy of my family.

"My boyfriend refuses to come, but I think the rest of us could use your help," I said.

"Grad students are supposed to handle student cases," he said. "But you have an interesting situation. I'll meet with your kids and both parents and we'll see how it goes."

\* \* \*

In June of 1985 Abstractions played at the State Fairgrounds in a Battle of the Bands final face-off with a three-sister group called the Fabulous Starlettes. The competition was sponsored by cable television and radio station 93FM WNAP. It was a challenging show because we took the stage at 2:00 on a Friday afternoon. It was disheartening to look out on the sparse crowd. People seemed just as interested in the tractor exhibit beyond the stage as they were in listening to us. Our biggest fans present were my sister Pam (who had long ago ripped through two marriages and was now dating our bass player, Rusty) her eighteen-year-old daughter, Beth, and a former Wonderwall customer and diehard band devoteé, Jill Kelly.

The Fabulous Starlettes who sang right-on Andrews Sisters harmonies won the competition, but we walked away with live videotape. The cable company filmed our set using three cameras and provided us with a copy of our vigorous performance.

During that same time, we were also invited to perform at the cable-access channel, along with some other local bands we'd never met.

"This could be a nightmare," Jack said. "I don't wanna take a bunch of guitars and equipment where other bands might end up ripping off our gear."

"That's right," Gesualdo said. "Remember what a hassle it was when we played with other bands at Slayter Center? That was a mess."

Oh yeah. I remembered the gig at Purdue's outdoor facility, Slayter Center. The student organizers met us in the late morning with beer kegs already tapped. We were the headliner and by the time we took the stage that evening I was a drunken mess. Thank God our sound-man was able to add effects to my voice to camouflage the slurring performance. Even though we'd spray painted a big green A (for Abstractions) on all our gear, we still lost some band equipment. With that vision in mind, I made a proposition.

"Why don't we just take a bunch of crap from the garage and play air guitar?" I said.

Everybody liked the idea of air guitar to my song, "Wah Wah." The short, skinny drummer Kevin wore my Michelin t-shirt and grabbed a bicycle pump. He kept time as he raised and lowered the handle. Jack rigged a sledgehammer with rope around his neck and 'played' the guitar with big thick work gloves covering his hands. The short-lived bass player member, Tony, used a broom variously as his 'axe' and a sweeping timepiece. Gesualdo donned an Indy 500 shirt under a paint-splattered blue jean shirt and jeans ensemble. Rather than emulate keyboard playing he flipped a piece of thick rubber hose in time to the music in a phallic gesture. Patty dressed in gray overalls and wrapped a red bandanna around the end of a crowbar. She placed her lips around the stick and pretended it was her sax. I dressed in

51

pink fishnet stockings, red heels, a lilac mini-skirt, sky blue spaghetti-strapped leotard and a purple hand-me-down Meryl Streep jacket Jack brought back from a family holiday. I danced among the tires and car repair miscellany as I 'sang' into a wooden handle. I glistened with the rhinestones that covered my jacket and thrift store jewels worn at my neck, ears, wrists and hands.

It was a blast throwing the lip-synched performance together and again we came away with a well-produced video of the event. We felt ready to finally work on the "real thing."

# 8

# I Want My MTV

I'd conjured up a new fantasy for myself. I now believed that music video could become my vehicle into acting and the film business. MTV was an exploding cultural phenomenon, and I envisioned great things for our band.

We hired a director named Carol Trexler to help us with the video project. I met at her home to discuss the details. She enlisted the help of a cameraman named Craig Somers.

"Craig's worked on several John Mellencamp videos, but wants the chance to be a chief cinematographer," Carol said. "He'll do your project for just his cost."

Because we were using 35mm film, the total budget was set at $10,000—- the same amount we'd spent on recording our EP.

"Unfortunately, my idea for a location has been shot down," Carol said."The city of Zionsville declined my request. I guess they don't want to be associated with rock video. Any ideas?"

I described the awesome house we were renting and said, "Maybe we can use the mansion."

"Pay us a dollar," said the owners. We signed a simple agreement and scheduled the shoot.

Jack prepared a silk screen and produced t-shirts for all the background people to wear. They were red or white with black letters reading Abstractions *Check It Out,* and a checkerboard pattern on the front.

My sister Pam re-styled an antique dress I'd gotten from Aunt Becky's estate for me to wear in some of the shots. Our dear friend and hairstylist Micheal Barnes agreed to be on hand for make-up and 'dos. The sax player Patty and I chose pink and plum same-styled cocktail dresses we'd found at the thrift store for the opening shots. She hiked hers up on one side for a sexy view of one leg.Eddy, with his Flock-of-Seagulls-flavored hair, was my sister's new crush, who finagled a brand-new van from the car dealer where his father worked.

Early on the morning of the shoot a huge truck pulled into the mansion driveway with a hundred thousand dollars' worth of gear. Craig brought a minimal crew to help with lighting and sound, but they were pros and handled everything we needed.

I like to describe the "Wah Wah" theme as typically Hoosier: "Girl is into boy who's into cars and sports."

We started in the front yard with our eighteen friends and family extras dancing in the background.

Landon, Gesualdo and some of the other guys appeared climbing from the van with softball equipment in one scene. Another showed them playing basketball behind the mansion and included a beautiful close-up of Landon's muscular, sexy torso glistening with actual sweat.

Gesualdo dressed as a mechanic and stuck his head under the van hood for some of the shots. He sauntered over to me as I pouted against the fender and offered me a peck on the cheek while he wiped imaginary grease from his hands. Craig also got a close, sexy shot of my curvaceous calf and windblown skirt as

I stood watching Gesualdo massage the side of the van with a rag.

After dark, we moved into the mansion to shoot me draped in a satin sheet against the sparkling mint green tile of the breakfast nook. Craig arranged powerful lights outside the windows to create the illusion of morning.

As we moved from shot to shot and one costume to the next, I slipped into my bedroom to take a few puffs on my pipe or slug a sip of beer. In the final hours of the long day, I was running out of steam, and we'd exhausted all my weed stash. Landon and his pals had polished off all the booze with ample help from the band.

As I stood waiting for the next shot Carol walked over from a tête-à-tête with Craig.

"You seem a little uptight," she said. "Is there anything available for you to drink or smoke?"

I felt ashamed because I didn't know she knew I was a party girl. It was also embarrassing to think she and Craig thought my acting looked stiff.

"Actually, no. There's nothing around," I admitted.

"Do your best to relax," she said. "Let's try this again. Roll film. Roll sound. Action!"

It was eleven o'clock when the massive truck pulled away from the mansion. We had our film. Now all we had to do was edit it down.

We spent three days sitting at the elbow of Gesualdo's high school friend, John Scofield, as he worked his editing magic. He inserted dissolves, fades, and precision cuts to match the beats of the dance song.

One major local television network invited me onto their show for an interview while the two others did live video feeds from the mansion lawn on the night of our release party.

Finally, with the finished product in our hands, I submitted it for MTV's Basement Tapes show. That show was a precursor to the current TV competition shows. MTV played videos from unknown bands, and the nationwide audience called in to vote for their favorite artist. Just a few days after I mailed the tape, I received a letter from the network.

"Thank you for your submission. It takes approximately six weeks for us to review your tape and respond.We will notify you if we decide to air your tape."

I was crushed. All that work. All that money. We'd spent $20,000 on the record and video and all we got was a generic rejection letter. I smoked a joint with Ricky as I recounted my sob story.

The next day the phone rang.

"We want to play your video on our next episode of the Basement Tapes," the lady said. "We're Fed Ex'ing the paperwork and releases. Please get them back to us right away."

# 9

# Binges and Evictions

Abstractions assembled for the signing of the paperwork. This was pre-internet, so almost every unknown band in the world wanted a chance to be seen on The Basement Tapes. Six chosen bands competed, with the winner earning a lousy record contract. Still, it was better than no contract at all, and we wanted to win.

By the time The Basement Tapes was scheduled to air we'd moved back to our new, remodeled house. Ken Gregory had exceeded our expectations. We knocked out the wall of the master bedroom's walk-in closet to create a new bedroom in the space above the two and a half-car garage. That room had a skylight, ceiling fan and sloped sidewalls. The old master bedroom space was converted to a TV room.

Gesualdo moved into the new, nine-hundred-square-foot room on the upstairs level.

"How much living space do we have now?" I asked Ken.

"Since your basement is also finished, we'd include that. Your total is about forty-four hundred square feet."

The house was now five levels with three and a half bathrooms.

We installed two skylights and two ceiling fans in Gesualdo's room, along with a full bath.

\* \* \*

"What do you want for Christmas?" asked Gesualdo's cousin, Aaron.

"A harpsichord," Gesualdo replied.

That had been his answer to any person asking that question for as long as I'd known him. Imagine our surprise when he opened a harpsichord ornament on Christmas Day.

"The Indianapolis Symphony is selling me their Wittmayer harpsichord for you," Aaron said.

It was a nine-foot harpsichord, so we moved that into the new upstairs bedroom. The Wittmayer instrument was built in Germany in the early sixties and debuted at Carnegie Hall. The symphony sold the keyboard to Aaron because the design included an electric amplification system some purist musicians found objectionable. When Gesualdo played it with the doors to his new room open, it sounded like angels in heaven wafting through the air.

Landon and I moved into the room above the garage, even though we were weathering some stormy times. During our stay in the mansion, it seemed as if Landon was drinking more than ever. One night he never made it home and I tossed and turned all night. I vacillated between fury and distress but became completely confused when I awoke the next day to find him sleeping in his car in the driveway.

"What the hell's your problem?" I demanded. "Why didn't you come in?"

"I didn't feel like it."

"Why are you drinking so much?"

"Whaddaya expect? You have me living in this fucked-up situation. You'd drink too if you was in my shoes."

He had a point. Maybe this was more than he could handle.

At the same time, I was starting to question my own pot smoking. It occurred to me that I'd been smoking daily for fifteen years. I told myself, "You've had your fun. So far, you don't have any arrests or diseases from all the years of smoking. Your dad's family has a history of heart disease. Shouldn't you quit while you're ahead?"

* * *

Once Landon and I started down the road of self-questioning, things between us continued to deteriorate. He began a pattern of closing the bars often—- followed by skipping work the next day. He was now laying sod for his stepfather's landscape company where they tolerated his poor attendance because he was a strong worker when he showed up. I was grossed out by his behavior and felt insecure that he would pick up women when he was drunk. While I was confident of Gesualdo's devotion, Landon's youth and supposed desire for a family threatened my security.

The worst nights were the ones when he still wasn't home by 3:00 a.m. I'd flail about, imagining disastrous scenarios and struggle with interrupted passages of sleep. If I had pot I could get out of bed, smoke a bowl and calm down enough to fall back asleep. When I ran out of reefer my feelings would escalate till I was sobbing and writing self-pitying poetry or packing

Landon's bags to throw him out. This happened repeatedly.

Landon had lived with us off and on for five years when I had an epiphany.

"You think he's an alcoholic?" I asked my favorite stoner girlfriend, Evelyn.

"Of course," she laughed. "Are you really just now figuring that out?"

Kyrie was now eleven years old and even she understood the routine. She was increasingly snotty and disrespectful toward me.

One day after a sleepless night of Landon's drinking I snapped at her to clean up her room and she shot back at me.

"Don't think you can order me around just because Landon won't do what you want."

I knew she was right, but I wasn't willing to overlook her hostile attitude toward the whole family.

"Why is Kyrie so mean to all of us?" Rena cried one day when her sister slammed a door in her face.

"She doesn't like Landon living with us," I explained.

"But he's nice. I like him."

Rena always accepted Landon more than Kyrie. He'd been in her life since age three. Kyrie blamed him for our abnormal household and barely spoke to him.

The therapist at Butler was working with Kyrie and me together, to help us through our battles. After several months he asked to speak with me alone.

"I'm going to terminate counseling Kyrie."

"Why? We're fighting more than ever."

"She's uncounselable. She criticizes and blames you and her father for all her misery. She refuses to accept responsibility for any of her own bad behavior."

It seemed obvious Kyrie was determined to make me suffer for the awkward household because she was embarrassed. I found out from other parents that she lied to her friends about the reality of our marriage, and I could see she tried to spend most of her time at their homes.

The whole vibe in our cool new house was lousy. Every one of my friends and family were fed up with my complaining about Landon's drinking. Finally, one day my older sister, Pam, came to visit and tossed a paperback book at me.

"Read this and do something." She ground her cigarette into the ashtray." Nobody wants to listen to any more of your crap. We're all sick of it."

I turned the book over and read the title Women Who Love Too Much. What did I have to lose? I read the damned book and was horrified to read the tales of women in toxic relationships. Many of them were far worse than Landon's and mine but I knew I also needed help. Each chapter seemed to end with "...and then she went to a recovery group." I'd never heard of recovery groups.

* * *

"It sounds as if Rosemary's upset," I said to Gesualdo one muggy night. From across the driveway, it sounded like she was yelling and throwing dishes or something.

"Yeh, she's been pretty sensitive since they decided to divorce again," he said. "She and her son will stay in the house."

Things between us had also worsened. I was grateful I could unload to the therapist.

"We were at a party last week and I walked into a drunk Gesualdo talking smack about me. That's never happened

61

before. No way I'm staying in the marriage if he's gonna punish me for a situation he agreed to up front. I think we should get a divorce," I said.

"Why? He lets you have your cake and eat it too. Isn't he going to be rich someday? Why would you leave?"

"I didn't marry him for his money. It would be slimy to stay married for that reason."

* * *

It was true Gesualdo and his two brothers were going to be well off. Their grandfather's sister, Aunt Becky, died in 1979. Her will distributed Blue Chip stocks to the three boys' families. A year later, their cousin Aaron disbursed the amazing wardrobes of his mother and Aunt Beck. Many of their clothes featured embroidered tags that read, "Especially made for Miss H. R. O. (or Mrs. H. L.) by the Hong Kong Tailor." The clothes-maker would come to Indianapolis, show the ladies designs and fabrics, and return to Hong Kong to build the wool coats, suits and brocade dresses. My sisters-in-law and I divided all the garments including piles of white gloves and various silk scarves. I also received large boxes filled with feather and wool hats and a dozen purses in every style and color from a beige leather bucket to coral satin and alligator bags. Three years later Aaron invited all the wives of Gesualdo and his brothers to divide the jewelry Aunt Becky left behind.

As I prepared to meet Aaron and the girls, I said, "There's only one thing I know I want. That yellow ring Aunt Becky wore all the time."

Susan (Kim's wife), Cindy (Jan's wife), and I met at Aaron's house on a sunny Saturday morning. Aaron seated us around the classy dining room table and presented a white alligator satchel filled with jewels. As he emptied the bag he'd tell the origin of each piece, who owned it, where it was bought, the occasion of the gift etc.

"We'll go in order," Aaron instructed. "Since Kim is oldest Susan will go first, Cindy will go next, and Joyce will go third. You'll each take one piece of jewelry until it's all gone."

By the time we started choosing, the table was covered with baubles. There were necklaces, bracelets, brooches, and rings. There were stones of every color, bug shaped pins, cameos, and pearls.

Susan gazed across the expanse of finery and finally made her choice. Cindy picked up a couple of pieces, returned them to their place and took a few deep breaths.

"So many beautiful things. It's hard to choose."

I was glancing around the room studying the gold-leaf wallpaper, the black lacquer oriental box and Waterford candlesticks on the buffet. Anything to keep myself from staring at the coveted yellow ring Aaron placed among the other treasures. At last, Cindy selected a cabochon sapphire ring.

"Are you finished?" I asked.

"I think so."

"Are you sure?"

She exhaled and beamed. "I'm sure."

I lunged at the table.

"I want this ring!"

Everyone sat back in their chairs at my abrupt movement. I immediately slipped the ring on my right-hand finger.

"I knew it would fit. I'm ecstatic."

Aaron said the citrine ring came from the antique jewelry

department at Cartier's in New York.

"If you take that ring you need to take this bracelet I bought to go with it," he said. It had gold bar links with nine 3/4" long oval citrines. I'd never seen the bracelet before.

"That's fine. I'll skip my next turn."

The amazing process continued for hours until every trinket was in the grateful hand of its new, appreciative owner. Once the table was empty Jack turned to the buffet. There he lifted three boxes and handed one to each of us.

"These are specific bequests."

I opened my box and gazed upon a single modern-styled gold pin with nine sparkling stones of various sizes ranging from .15 points to .75 carats.

"Are these diamonds?"

"Yes," Aaron answered.

"I've never owned a diamond."

"Aunt Beck knew that."

As I headed to my car, the last one to leave, Aaron walked with me. He held the door open as I slid inside with my mundane, grubby shorts I'd donned for this occasion.

"You're going to be very rich someday. Just be good," he said.

Cindy always insisted Aaron gave us the jewels as a form of hush money to make amends for an ugly secret inside this wealthy, but sincerely generous, family.

\* \* \*

Aaron's words echoed in my mind as I drove away from the therapist where I'd just announced my intention to divorce. I hadn't been anyone's definition of good for a very long time.

In fact, I'd been out raising hell the night before the jewelry distribution. I didn't deserve a share of Gesualdo's future family riches.

# 10

# Venture Capital, Anyone?

"If we're divorcing, we need to decide how to separate all the stuff we've accumulated," Gesualdo said as we sat across from each other in the TV room.

I grabbed a legal pad, and we walked through the five levels of our spectacular home. We made a list of all the things each of us would take, without argument.

By this time our large house was full of furniture, paintings, musical instruments, and hundreds of vinyl records. Since most of our valuables were inherited and neither of us thought of ourselves as particularly materialistic, the process was painless. I would get the rock and roll; he'd take the classical records. I'd take the DeGrazias, he'd keep the Diego Riveras. We were finished with the list in just a single hour. As we stood in the entryway giving it one last look, Gesualdo stunned me.

"How about moving to California so you can act?"

I'd been waiting fifteen years for the chance to do that very thing. Now he was willing? I didn't know how to respond. My first thought was to wonder what he'd do about his job as the treasurer of his family's business.

"Let me think about it. How can you leave T&L?"

"I'm willing to leave if we just forget about getting divorced."

As I contemplated moving away with him and the kids, fear engulfed me. What if I couldn't bear to be apart from Landon? What if Gesualdo harbored resentment for the six years of marital chaos and never let me forget it? What if we were no longer exclusively sexually compatible? After just two days I thanked him for the offer but told him I'd pass.

We sat down with Kyrie and Rena in the living room and explained our decision.

"I'm only nine years old and you're already getting divorced?" Rena cried.

Kyrie also burst into tears.

"But why?" she asked. "You've never even had an argument."

It was true the girls hadn't seen us squabble. We'd kept our few disagreements behind closed doors. Kyrie didn't wait for an answer to her question. She spun around, stomped up the stairs, and slammed her door. It was heartbreaking to see the kids so upset, but I still believed we'd finally made a correct decision. Her father followed Kyrie upstairs and talked quietly with her as I held Rena and tried to calm her down.

Gesualdo surprised me again by announcing a few days later that he'd rented an apartment and was moving immediately. He also contacted an attorney, filed for divorce, and started meeting with his family members to finally tell them the truth about our marriage.

\* \* \*

As my home-life unraveled, I began planning to support myself.

After completing my master's degree, I was hired to teach public speaking at Indiana University-Purdue University at Indianapolis (IUPUI). Through their "Learn and Shop" program I was teaching communications classes in the training room of JC Penney's at one mall and Sears at another. It was fun and invigorating work, and it made me feel as if I were doing an important "grown up" job.

Abstractions fell apart; Eddy left us for the Fabulous Starlettes (and married my sister), Jack was suffering with serious back problems, Kevin married, and his wife was expecting a baby, Patty left (with an apparent broken heart) to get away from Jack, and everybody in the band seemed fed up with me bossing them around, pushing for more performances.

Amid the bedlam, I had an idea for a new creative project. We purchased the video rights for the Stones tune "The Last Time" for $500. I wanted to make a new video and thought MTV would surely play it if we covered the Rolling Stones song we'd included on our *Check It Out* EP.

Craig Somers from the "Wah Wah" video said he'd be interested in working with us again but wanted a $20,000 budget for the new song.

With the divorce underway and most of Aunt Becky's money long gone on band equipment and the previous recording projects, we couldn't afford to finance the video ourselves.

I attended several seminars on raising venture capital and decided to write a business plan.

"It should take about three hundred hours to create a professional plan that would attract backers," the fired-up instructor said.

Step one required creating a board of directors for our company. We were advised to have an Eagle Scout on the board.

Check. Gesualdo was an Eagle Scout. I met a guy, Greg Brown, at the venture capital seminars who agreed to join our board as an "idea man." Greg owned a design company in Lafayette. Next, I enlisted a partner from the largest independent accounting firm in Indiana, Dave Schmitt from Geo. S. Olive & Co. Gary Schatzlein, the owner of TRC recording studios also came on board as did Robin Moore, a sales rep. from a local radio station.

Step two took about six months as I wrote the plan including marketing ideas and possible sales projections. My sister helped immensely with her 120+ WPM typing skills. Once the plan was finished, I submitted a synopsis to the Venture Club of Indiana and requested a presentation slot at their monthly meeting.

"You will be one of three presenters and have seven minutes to make your pitch," they replied.

Step three involved showing up at the meeting and giving them my spiel. I used proven public speaking preparation skills like the ones I taught every week. I rehearsed over and over to condense my talk into just 3 1/2 minutes, so I could play the "Wah Wah" video for the rest of my allotted time. I arrived at the luncheon and looked down to see the stack of business plan outlines for distributing, and the videotape for playing. I'd left the notecards for my speech at home!

# 11

# Reality is for People Who Can't Handle Drugs

My endless rehearsals paid off. I breezed through my pitch and rolled the videotape.The venture capitalists burst into a standing ovation then sat again to listen to the other two presenters talk about their soybean product ideas or something. I was deaf with nerves and excitement. Gesualdo and I soaked up praise and compliments, but not a single serious investor inquiry.

With the prospect of financing for more music projects dead as flattened roadkill, I felt agitated and disconnected with my Indy life. My divorce from Gesualdo was finalized, and I was now a regular at recovery meetings.

I liked the program's slogans. They were nothing unique that I hadn't heard all my life, but in the context of learning to be a better person, they sounded fresh. I swam at the IUPUI lap pool twice a week, and repeated the slogans in my mind as I swam, "Live and Let Live", "Let Go and Let God", "First Things First." People in the meetings told me to visit open alcoholic recovery meetings so I could learn to "understand and encourage the alcoholic."

"I know you want a family. You should find a partner who's willing to do that," I said to Landon.

"I wanna be with you. Let's you and me get married," he said.

"You keep messing around and you're gonna find yourself alone," Mother warned me.

That thought was terrifying. Soooo, I shopped for a wedding gown, reserved a reception hall, planned catering and a ceremony at the Unitarian Church. Landon and I took my pin from Aunt Becky to his cousin's jewelry store.

"Let's use the largest diamond in a necklace for your engagement," Landon said. We chose a simple setting that really set off the three-quarter carat stone.

He ordered a channel set ring to hold the half-carat diamond to serve as my wedding ring. We chose October tenth as our nuptial date and began preparing guest lists.

\* \* \*

It was a Saturday and Landon went with his buddy Glen to the Indianapolis Indians' Bush Stadium to watch some sporting event. We planned a barbecue with Glen and his girlfriend Betty for later in the evening. They were a handsome young couple who only recently entered the workforce. The expected time for the guys to return home came and went, as I got more and more annoyed. When they arrived 2 hours late, Landon's car was smashed in the front left quarter panel. He was drunk, but laughing as he recounted the story about hitting a guardrail while entering the freeway.

"I looked away away to light my cigarette and got a little too close."

"Well at least nobody was hurt," I said.

Betty and I were ready to start dinner, but the guys wanted to run to the store for more beer.

"Don't you think you've had enough?" I asked, forgetting everything I'd learned in recovery. That group believes a person should never confront a loved one who's been drinking.

"We're just having a good time," Landon said as he threw his arms around my neck and laid a big, boozy kiss on my lips.

"Don't be such a party pooper. Forget the barbecue. Let's go to the racetrack. Dad's driving tonight." Landon's father was a regular competitor who specialized in driving the risky and difficult Crazy 8 race.

Now I was freaked. The last time he went drunk to watch his dad race, Landon got in a shoving match with another loudmouth. While Landon and Glen made the beer run, I got on the phone to Landon's friend, Ricky.

"Can you come over and talk sense to him? He listens to you better than me when he's loaded."

"You know how he is, Joyce. If he wants to leave, nobody's really gonna stop him. But I can come over and see what's up."

When he came in the house, Landon put the beer in the fridge and threw his keys on the table.

"I gotta pee like a racehorse."

The minute he rounded the corner to the bathroom I snatched the keys and threw them in my purse. Betty had diverted Glen and was whispering to him out at the picnic table. Landon came out of the bathroom, grabbed a beer for himself, handed me one and took one for Glen. We walked out into the yard as Glen and Betty stood up. Glen waved off the beer.

"No, thanks, man. I'm pretty fucked up already. I think we're just gonna take off."

Betty was driving because Glen lost his license in a recent DUI. I walked over to hug her goodbye and whispered, "Thanks. Maybe if Glen isn't with him, Landon'll skip the track idea."

No sooner had they pulled away when Landon walked back inside. I jumped on the kids' swing and was pumping away when he returned.

"Where's my keys? I wanna get to the track before Dad's first race."

"I dunno. Maybe you left 'em in your car."

I'm a terrible liar. I can never sound innocent if I'm trying to pull a fast one. I figured if I focused on swinging, I could distract Landon from my dishonesty. He went over to the driveway and looked inside his car but was back again to question me.

"Stop screwing around. Gimme my keys."

I dragged my feet in the grass and stopped the swing.

"I don't have your stupid keys. Maybe it's best anyway. It's not like you should really be driving anywhere in the shape you're in."

"Don't piss me off, Joyce."

With that, he stomped back into the house, leaving the door ajar. He went from room to room, searching every table and countertop.

A loud BANG jolted me out of the swing.

I raced to the garage and saw Landon holding his right hand in his left. There was a big hole in the wall where his fist had punched it.

"Give me my goddamned keys! This is all your fault."

"You know what? You're insane," I said.

Just then I saw Ricky pull into the driveway. I opened the garage door and ran over to his car.

"Please take this maniac out of here. He's tearing up my

73

house!" I yelled.

Ricky lit a cigarette and walked over to look at Landon's hand. As they stood in the driveway, I shut the garage door and locked the back door of the house. Then I ran to the front door and locked that one, too. I trembled, dreading what else Landon might do. I set the burglar alarm and went upstairs to watch the guys from the window.

"Come on, man, let's just get out of here," Rick said.

"No fucking way. She can give me my fucking keys so I can go watch Dad race," Landon hollered.

Rick had his hand on Landon's shoulder when Landon pulled away and headed for my front door.

He rang the doorbell maniacally, which I ignored. Then he began pounding on the door with his fist. I shouted through the door.

"Give it up, Landon. Just leave. I've set the alarm and you're not getting in here."

"You BITCH!"

With that, he kicked the door with all his might, then turned to split. I heard him slam Rick's car door as he got inside, and they drove away. I went into my room, smoked a bowl of dope and waited for my heart to stop hammering.

I went down the stairs, turned off the alarm and looked at my front door. A piece of the trim was broken and hanging loose. I went back to the garage, looked at the hole in the wall, then walked back inside, sank down on the couch and tears poured out of me.

# 12

# Moving On

Suddenly I had an experience recovery groups call a "moment of clarity." It occurred to me that I was making a huge mistake. I was about to marry a man whose life was a mess. He could barely work, drank too much, and had just wrecked his car and torn up my house in a single day. This wasn't the first time Landon had struck inanimate objects.

He suffered what I called "Jack attacks" after drinking Jack Daniels. He put a hole in the dining room wall once, the master bedroom wall once, and his car's windshield another time. Each of the times he tore up a wall of our house, I demanded he make it better than before. He hung beautiful wallpaper to cover the holes, but it was a reminder of his drunken violence.

I reached out to my gal pal. "Holy crap, Evelyn, marrying Landon could be a gigantic monetary catastrophe. I might be giving up my home and financial stability. Loving him is not enough. I need to cancel the wedding."

"That's probably a good call," she said.

To strengthen my resolve, I went to my family recovery meeting the next night where I got support from the people who really understood my painful decision. They let me cry and listened to the three-minute version of my sob story when it was my turn to share.

Landon finally called Monday evening.

"The wedding is off," I said. "The bridal shop said I can pick any other dress from their store. The church, reception hall and caterer are all notified. I told your cousin to size the wedding ring for my right hand and bought you a gold nugget. I cancelled your ring and put the two diamonds planned for it in the nugget with a gold chain."

"Please don't do this, Joyce," Landon said when we finally got together. "I promise I'll quit drinking. I'm so sorry!"

Knowing my decision was final, I felt calm.

"I know you're sincere and you think you'll stop," I said. "We've been through this too many other times. I just can't take a chance on risking everything. I still absolutely love you and hope we can work this out. I need to see you with at least a year of sobriety before I plan a wedding."

I handed him the jewelry box as I continued. "I want you to wear this necklace and remember what Bruce Springsteen says—-'two hearts are better than one.' I really hope maybe someday we'll be married."

* * *

Recovery altered my life. The program taught me that I needed to take my eyes off the alcoholic and look at myself. I continued visiting alcoholic recovery meetings, hoping I could increase my understanding of the disease of alcoholism. The stories of the participants were disturbing. People's lives were damaged and pathetic, yet I heard them express hope for a better future. I got a recovery mentor, Cheryl, who started taking me through the program of action — - based on alcoholics' recovery program.

After I admitted I was powerless over alcohol, (and all other people, places, things, and situations) and that my life had become unmanageable, I got to step two. It said, "Came to believe that a power greater than myself could restore me to sanity." Whoa. Inherent in that step was acknowledgment that I was not sane.

"Doing the same thing over and over, but expecting different results is how we define insanity," Cheryl told me.

The endless cycle of Landon's and my break-ups and reconciliations qualified for that one. It was comforting to know I might find my way back to sanity. My brother, Gary, had been telling me for years that I was nuts. I disregarded it as sibling sniping, but maybe he had a point.

Another recovery concept says, "Became willing to turn our will and our lives over to the care of God, as we understood God." The idea of deciding my own concept of God was consistent with Unitarian Universalism. Even though I never considered myself a religious person and rarely used the word God, the third step was ok with me.

"Tell me about your religious upbringing," Cheryl said.

"Mother and Dad each abandoned their religions when they married. Mother was raised Mormon, while Dad's family was Catholic. I attended the Protestant Youth of the Chapel group when I lived in Germany because all the cutest guys went there. I shopped all the youth groups when I moved to Indiana, looking for the biggest party group. Of course, I've now been a practicing Unitarian for many years."

As I got more involved with recovery, making friends, attending consistent meetings, and working the steps, I felt more stable and stronger. I decided I would move to California on my own.

A phone call to Dick, an old high school friend, now a successful realtor, got my house on the market.

"Because you're the biggest house in the neighborhood, we'll be lucky to get $105,000," Dick said.

At the same time, I also returned to therapy. This time I sought out a female therapist and found a petite brunette, Laura.

"If you're coming here every week and spending all this money to get better, I need you to do a few things," she told me at the first session."First of all, I need you to read The Road Less Traveled by M. Scott Peck. Next, I need you to stop using all drugs and alcohol. The purpose of therapy is to get to the truth. If you are drinking and using drugs, we'll never get to the truth. Are you willing to do these things?"

"I'm absolutely willing to read the book. I don't know about the drinking and drugs. I don't drink that much, but I really love smoking pot."

"Well, I want you to commit to stop during the time we work together."

"I'll give it my best shot," was the best I could manage.

# 13

# California Dreamin'

The book blew my mind. Scott Peck talked about the evolution of long-term relationships in a language I'd never heard. He pointed out the difference between love and something called cathexis. As I understood it, one could have feelings of adoration for objects or ideas (cathexis), but love was different. He discussed growing apart from his wife, over time, but suggested that couples could rekindle their feelings of love if they were truly interested in staying committed and helping their partner to grow spiritually.

I felt as if I'd blown my life. It seemed obvious that the information might have helped or encouraged me to stay in my marriage with Gesualdo. Too bad our divorce was final, and he'd moved in with Rosemary.

Another shock. Who knew I couldn't stop drinking and smoking? I'd made countless resolutions to stop getting high over the course of the previous five years, but always started again. I honestly thought it was a conscious decision to change my mind. Now I had the embarrassing experience of facing my therapist, Laura, week after week, making endless excuses about why I was unsuccessful stopping.

"I didn't buy any dope, does that count? I only had one beer at the David Bowie concert. I just had two hits off a joint." Etc., etc.

I was secretly horrified that I couldn't go an entire week without drinking or smoking. I never really knew at my core of being that I drank and smoked because I was "...powerless over alcohol..." as the first recovery suggestion says.

The next sly thing Laura did was ask me to write the history of my relationship with Gesualdo. I wrote a shortened version of this book and obediently brought it to her comfortable suburban office.

"Good," she said. "Read it to me."

I wanted to crawl under the chair! There's no way I expected to have to say what I'd written aloud. I sat there uncomfortable and self-conscious but read it to her anyway.

"Did you notice how much of your own drinking and using is in this?" she asked when I finished.

I felt my face flush. "Not really," I said, wondering what she was talking about.

"Have you ever had sex without drugs or alcohol?"

"Of course!"

Again, I felt insulted and ashamed that she could even think such a thing.

"Next week I want you to bring me the history of your relationship with Landon," Laura said at the end of the session.

I'm sure I was more careful writing that version since I now knew what would be coming next. The following week when I finished reading the Landon chronicle Laura said, "That's important recovery work you've finished. You're ready to move on with the rest of your program."

When I first contacted Laura, I didn't realize she was sober twelve years in the program for recovering alcoholics. After I learned her status as a sober woman, I thought it was probably a lucky coincidence. People in alcoholic recovery groups sometimes suggest God might have a hand in random helpful events.

"Is that odd or is that God?" is the expression.

The combination of therapy and the actions of the program brought me to a new realization. I finally realized I needed to do something about my own drinking and using.

\* \* \*

My house sold, I put everything into storage and was now living with my parents, as I finished teaching the semester of classes at IUPUI. I contacted an old college friend, Margene Chrisman, who lived in Ontario, California.

"Do you have room for an extra person?" I asked.

"Absolutely. Jeremy and I are in a three-bedroom townhome, so you're welcome to stay as long as you like."

I admired Margene who had raised Jeremy by herself. She put herself through an MBA program while always providing a nurturing home for her brilliant, strong, redheaded son. She worked hard as a director of operations for a retail clothing supplier while maintaining the effort to improve her standard of living.

I could barely wait to wrap up all my commitments in Indy so I could start my new life in California.

"You girls are gonna love it!" I said.

"Actually, Mom, we're staying here in Indy with Dad," Kyrie

said.

"Rosemary and I have plenty of room in our new house," Gesualdo said.

"Has it occurred to you that they may just prefer the stability of being with their Dad? They know you smoke pot every day and may be sick of all the craziness you create," Laura said at the next therapy session.

"Oh my God, that's horrible!" I said.

I drove home in a daze.

\* \* \*

I made appointments at every doctor and dentist for final checkups and planned to COBRA my health insurance.

"Make sure you check your thyroid," Mother said. "I think you might be having a problem. Your eyes don't look right."

# 14

# New Face, New Body, New Life

The most recent photos of myself showed my eyes bulged out, but I thought the pictures were just lousy. I'd also been gaining weight and now weighed 157 pounds — - more than I weighed at the term of my two pregnancies. I drank Slim Fast but was having no luck dropping any of the weight.

"Please just check my thyroid so I can humor mother," I told the handsome Dr. Sharp. He'd been my doctor for Kyrie's delivery and had remained the kids' pediatrician.

He called the next day.

"Mother's right," he began. "You need to see an endocrinologist. Your thyroid levels are elevated."

When I arrived at the next doctor's office, he greeted me with a handshake.

"You're very hyperactive," he said.

"How do you know?" I asked.

"Your body temperature is high. We'll get you taken care of. Trust me. It's a good thing you went into your doctor. This is a dangerous condition."

He determined that I had Graves' disease. His questionnaire

asked if I'd noticed my heart beating. I had. It asked if I'd felt hot. That was going on for months and I needed a fan blowing on me in the middle of winter at work. Was I aware that I was speaking fast? I always did, but I noticed most of the foreign students had dropped my class this semester. Perhaps I was talking at a faster pace than usual. The worst thing was when I tilted my head back and felt along my throat. There was a big lump where goiters are pictured in health books. I had no idea all the things happening to me were symptoms of a disease. Then he lowered the boom.

"It doesn't matter what you eat, or how much you exercise. You won't be able to do anything about your weight right now. Your metabolism is completely out of balance. Many people get very thin when they have Graves', but it sometimes manifests as it has in you.They get insatiable appetites and out-eat the thyroid."

Great, I thought. Here I am moving to California where looks are everything, but I look like an overweight, googly eyed freak. Perfect.

Over the course of the next few months, I concluded my college teaching assignment, said farewells to friends and family, and was treated for the Graves'. The doctor recommended drinking radioactive iodine that could kill the thyroid (inconsequential, he said), fix it, or cause me to go into hypo-activity.

"You'll know if you become hypo because you'll start experiencing achy joints and knees. Let me know if that happens because we'll have to put you on synthetic thyroid pills, probably for the rest of your life. They're very inexpensive and have few, if any, side effects."

I trusted the doctor completely and did precisely what he

recommended. I drank the radio-iodine potion even though it was served from a lead-lined goblet by a technician wearing elbow high space-age gloves. I was told not to pick up any babies for three days because they should not be exposed to the chemical I ingested. The doctor insisted it's a peculiar phenomenon—- only the thyroid absorbs the tonic. It doesn't affect other organs during normal body processing.

One day as I walked down a street, I suddenly felt severe strain in my knees. When I arrived at the doctor's office he shook my hand, as he had that first time we met.

"Just as I suspected," he said. "You're now hypo. Your body temperature is very low. Let's get some blood tests."

* * *

Rena was spending the summer at the Turquoise Trail (female group of the Prairie Trek Expedition) —- a semi-scientific New Mexico camp.

"Her diabetes has been difficult since puberty" Gesualdo said. "At camp her group will be out in the desert for weeks at a time, and medical help won't be readily available."

"I hope the sink-or-swim situation will encourage Rena to get back in control of her disease," I said.

* * *

"Let's take a road trip before I leave," I said to Kyrie. "I'll take you to Myrtle Beach, South Carolina for a week."

I was hoping we could make some needed repairs to our

strained relationship before I left town.

Kyrie got behind the wheel, put a Michael Jackson cassette on the stereo and drove the first few miles. As we crossed the state line to Ohio, she asked me to grab her purse.

"Can you get my lip gloss?"

I opened the purse and started searching. The first thing I touched was a package of birth control pills! I felt a jolt in my chest, as my mind raced.

"If I say something, we'll probably get into a shouting match and be off to a terrible start."

I took a breath, set the pills aside and continued looking for the lip gloss.

# 15

# Living Alone

At the same moment, Kyrie must have remembered that the pills were on top of her belongings.

"You know what? Never mind. I'm ok," she said.

"No problem. Your lip gloss is right here," I answered, handing her the tube. The recovery slogan had worked—-"Live and let Live."

The days in South Carolina seemed long and awkward. Our mediocre motel was near the beach, but not oceanfront. Kyrie and I had little to say to each other, and she was even reluctant to lie in a lounge chair near where I sat.

Our final night I bought tickets for the carnival rides on the boardwalk, hoping we could finalize our trip with an evening of revelry. The first ride Kyrie chose was a Gravitron—-a standing-up enclosed circle that tilted and spun. We laughed and screamed as we were jolted and jostled from our strapped positions.

When the ride stopped, Kyrie noticed that her purse had dumped behind her standing platform. An attendant came over, released the cushion, and began reaching for her belongings.

He handed out her wallet, lip gloss and then pulled his hand out with his mouth in a big O. Displayed between his outstretched fingers were the birth control pills I'd discovered that first day of our trip. Kyrie jumped to retrieve them as I doubled over with laughter. She wasn't laughing. She grabbed the rest of her stuff, and we jumped off the ride. Again, I chose to say nothing about the pills.

"How about the bumper cars next?" I asked.

"Fine."

"My stomach hurts," she said when that ride ended.

No doubt, it did. We gave away the rest of our tickets, but it was still early.

"Why don't we do some shopping?" I said.

"Fine."

I led the way to the department store lingerie section.

"I noticed your bras are too small," I said. "When I took the pill, I had to go up to a bigger bra size.Let's get you some new ones."

I could see by the scowl on her face that she didn't appreciate me mentioning the pill, but she selected a few new bras, without discussion. After we returned to the motel, I turned on the new Jane Pauley TV show called Real People. It felt comforting to have the familiar voice of my old high school friend in the room.

Kyrie went down to the phone booth to call her boyfriend, Travis. As I watched her in the lighted booth below our window, I imagined that was one fascinating conversation.

From that point on, Kyrie didn't speak to me. She laid in the back seat while I drove us to Atlanta to stay an evening with my friend, Delores and her two kids. Delores and I were now both divorced, each with two young daughters. They gave us a whirlwind mini tour of vibrant Atlanta and we headed home to

Indiana the next morning.

Again, Kyrie opted for the back seat, and feigned sleep for the entire 533 miles. As we neared my parents' house, Kyrie bolted up.

"Mom, please don't tell Dad or Grandma about the pills, ok?"

"There's no need to tell your grandmother, but your Dad will be responsible for you when I'm living twenty-five hundred miles away. He needs to know what's going on with you."

"Ok, but let me tell him," she said. "Please."

I wasn't sure we'd accomplished what I hoped to with that trip, but I wasn't sorry I'd tried. Maybe learning about the true nature of her relationship with Travis was the most important thing I needed to know about my daughter as I moved across the country. Her boyfriend was two years older, movie star handsome and had been voted "Most likely to be a centerfold" by his classmates. The seniors had willed him a "girlfriend old enough to drive" in their senior wills. I considered taking the two of them out for a nice dinner, so I could thank them for not making me a grandmother at age forty.

* * *

My final days in Indy were a repeat of the series of events with Landon. We rarely saw each other, my heart was aching, and he was drinking as much as ever. To alleviate my boredom and to get out of my parents' house, I went to a Parents Without Partners dance my final weekend in town. It was held at the Holiday Inn banquet room with plenty of drinking and a crowd of mostly-anxious-looking singles. One tall, slender guy seemed to be the big lady killer in the room. He wasn't particularly good looking, nor was he the best dancer, but women were lined up to dance with him. His name was Bill, and at the end of the night he asked if I'd like to go for coffee. We sat across from each other at a Denny's restaurant and I blathered something about recovery.

"The thing I love about my program," he began.

"What program are you talking about?" I said.

"Oh, I'm eight years sober in an alcoholic recovery group. The thing I love about my program is the honesty," Bill said.

It was as if a neon light flashed on for me. It had been years since I thought of myself living an honest life. In that moment I decided I would not look for a marijuana dealer when I reached California. It was going to be hard enough to accomplish my goal of becoming a working actress in LA without risking making a fool of myself by being a stoner. I would try to get sober.

\* \* \*

Landon stayed with me at my parents' that last night in town. Our final good-bye felt familiar, but un-special. Still, I didn't know how I could survive without him, and wondered if I'd ever see him again.

"Dad and I will drive with you across the country," Mother said. "We'll take a carload of your stuff and lead the way. Your Father got CB radios for both of us so we can communicate, if necessary."

Gary was now working as a sales representative for Warner Bros. Records, and he gave me boxes of leftover promotional cassettes for the trip.

"These are new releases," he said. "You won't like all of them, but they should help keep you awake."

The miles seemed endless. Some of the tunes were amazing finds like Red Earth, a cassette by an unfamiliar band called Crash Vegas, or Compositions by Anita Baker. Others stank up the car so much I could hardly wait to hurl them in the trash at the next rest stop.

Each evening I got my own motel room and collapsed when we finished the day's drive. I brought no weed, nor did I drink in the evenings when we stopped.

Dad's idea of travel was to start before dawn, drive eight or ten hours and crash after an early dinner. We arrived in Ontario, California on Sunday, August 5,1990.

Margene's adorable parents, tiny Norma and brawny Earl, joined Margene, Jeremy, my folks and me for a scrumptious barbecue lunch at Joey's—-one of their favorite eateries. My Dad and Earl were immediate fast friends and had the same easy Hoosier manner about them as we sat on the wooden benches with our service flags raised and waited for the juicy ribs and marshmallow-dripping yams to arrive. I was envious that Margene had persuaded her folks to follow her to California and understood at my deepest core that I was going to miss my family.

* * *

No sooner had my parents pulled away when I asked Margene for a phone book. I flipped through the pages as if it were a life-or-death matter until I found what I was looking for—- a recovery group for addicts. As I traveled the miles to California, I became uneasy about being able to stay away from pot. I worried that it was a big mistake leaving my weed stash with Landon for his friends. By the time I reached Margene's I was terrified. I was afraid alcoholic recovery groups wouldn't work for me because I didn't drink every day. I'd never heard of addiction groups, but there they were. I called the number listed and found out there was a meeting later that evening.

I established a routine for my first months in the state. Margene worked every day, but I'd get up early, too. In fact, I was having trouble sleeping. Later I learned that my experiences were part of the detoxification process most addicts go through.

I wanted to get in shape, so I used Margene's workout videos every day, but also noticed I was perspiring profusely. Most days, I took two showers because I couldn't stand my sweaty self.

People at addiction recovery meetings told me that if I drank or used drugs every day, I needed to go to a meeting every day. That was a relief for me to hear. What else did I have to do? I wasn't working and my head was as busy as a California freeway. Each day I'd go to at least one meeting. Some days it was family recovery, others it was groups for addicts and still other times I'd go to alcoholics' groups. People in the rooms told me that we "don't take anything that affects us from the neck up, including alcohol", but I continued drinking.

Margene sometimes drank wine with dinner or margaritas when we went out for Mexican food. It was nice having drinks with my old gal-pal. The thing is, I was now drinking more than ever. Margene might have a flute of champagne; I'd finish off the bottle.

One weekend Margene, her mother and I took a trip to Catalina Island, and I noticed I stayed drunk most of the time. Catalina is a popular destination for honeymooners or couples celebrating anniversaries. I felt like we were the only three women on the island who were unaccompanied by adoring companions. I was miserable and lonely, so I drowned my sorrow in tequila.

When we returned to Ontario, besides going to meetings, I was also busy establishing myself in acting classes and preparing to earn a living. I was accepted into Jeff Corey's acting classes in Malibu. I'd read that Jeff taught Jack Nicholson, Dustin Hoffman and other stars. He'd also just appeared in the film Bird on a Wire with Mel Gibson. The class was seventy-five miles from Margene's place, and I went faithfully once each week, but my performance work was inconsistent. Some weeks I'd get positive feedback on the scene I presented; other times Jeff blasted my acting.

"I need to see more of you in the work," he'd say. "You're a much more interesting person than the character I see in your scene."

One day I sobbed as I drove the entire seventy-five miles home. We'd spent the day doing improvisation in class, and I knew I sucked. Once I regained my composure, I called Jeff.

"I'm newly sober and I just don't know if I can act without smoking pot," I told him as I wept.

"I don't think it has anything to do with being sober. I've told you; your work is best when it reflects more of your actual personality. You've done a magnificent job with your voice. If you are truly talented, you should be able to stay sober and still act."

He said if. My confidence took another dive. Maybe he doesn't think I'm talented at all, I thought. I continued studying with Jeff for several more months, but when I'd been in California five months, I started to worry about the drive. I regularly passed accidents with mangled cars on my long commutes to and from

Malibu, and decided it was a warning that I should move closer to the city.

I called about an apartment that sounded perfect, but when I met the landlady for a tour of the place, she called me over to a small duplex across the street from where I was peering through the window. She looked me up and down before we went through the door.

"I don't think this will work for you," she warned.

I walked through the tiny unit and was repulsed when I saw a dirt floor in the bathroom!

"Do you have anything else?" I asked. I had no other prospects.

"Follow me."

I rented her one-bedroom apartment in North Hollywood for $475 per month ($15 more than my mortgage in Indy). It was across the street from a twenty-five-acre park, so I told myself the size of the place didn't matter.

As I sat in the small, dark apartment that first night, I had an epiphany. I was forty years old and was living alone for the very first time. I'd gone from my parents' home to the dorm, to my marriage, and then Marlene's. I had no idea whether I could handle living on my own.

# 16

# Teacher, Teacher

My first week in California, I traveled down to the Los Angeles Unified School District to apply for a job as a substitute teacher. I called them before I left Indy and brought all the required documentation. They needed my transcripts from Purdue and Butler, two letters of recommendation, and a copy of my teaching credential.

Even though I'd been working in the head shop and rock bands, I'd always kept my teaching credential current. After eight hours under the fluorescents at district headquarters, I'd passed an exam called the mini-C-BEST (California Basic Education Skills Test), gone through a three-person interview, and was given the final clearance requirements. I got the schedule for full-blown CBEST exams, gave them my fingerprints, and was told they'd be calling me to sub. Weeks went by, but the phone didn't ring.

\* \* \*

I was working occasional humbling jobs as an extra in film and

TV. Extras are the background actors who make it look as if scenes are taking place in real offices, stores or clubs. The pay was lousy ($40 per day) unless I worked more than eight hours. If I was lucky enough to work twelve or fourteen hours, it was decent money—- (time and a half up to ten, double time after that), but exhausting. I had to provide my own chair (to sit on when I wasn't on stage), clothing and make-up. Extras are fed after all the stars, other cast members, and crew. Still, I liked spending time on sets—- watching the acting process. I was running through my savings at a frightening clip.

Getting started as an actor is an expensive proposition. I had to pay for headshots, dues for joining the American Federation of Television and Recording Artists (AFTRA) and the Screen Actors Guild (SAG). I had trouble finding an agent who wanted to represent a (now) forty-one-year-old woman with no Hollywood acting credits. One SAG seminar presenter noted that only eight percent of acting jobs went to women in their forties! The odds were really discouraging—- and I still looked like Marty Feldman. My thyroid was fine, but my eyes were still bulging. I didn't have enough confidence to go out in clubs as a stand-up comic making fun of my own appearance.

Desperation can lead to creativity. I started doing self-promotion for substitute teaching work. I got up early, went to a high school main office dressed for work, and sat there while teachers signed in. I gave out my name and number to anyone who would take it, and the phone started to ring. I signed up to teach in English, PE and Special Education classes. Soon, I was working most days. I learned that certain schools had a hard time finding subs. They were in gang-infested neighborhoods where I was instructed by the sub-unit not to wear certain colors of clothing. I cheerfully took every assignment that was offered.

\* \* \*

I was still attending plenty of alcoholic recovery meetings. Two weeks into my addiction group tenure, a guy named Neal invited me to coffee. I ordered a cup of herbal tea and was shocked when he suddenly told me what was on his mind.

"You can't keep coming to our meetings if you're gonna keep drinking," Neal said. "You and your little pot problem. Why don't you come back when you get a real drug? If we drink, we're back smoking crack or slamming heroin. You put all of us at risk when you come to meetings after drinking."

I was stunned. I didn't know anybody was aware that I was still drinking. I brushed my teeth, chewed gum and thought I was being discreet. Neal continued.

"It's all the same problem. You say you want to stay away from pot, but you give yourself permission to still drink."

"I never drank that much," I said. "I could go for days or weeks without a drink."

"So, you were a periodic drinker. Ok, then picture this. You're out at a club, you've had a few brewskies, and someone comes up and asks you to go burn one. Will you be able to stay sober off pot if you've been drinking?"

I started laughing.

"I see what you're saying."

I got it. It made perfect sense. Of course, I could see myself getting loaded if I were already loose with booze.

"Besides," he went on. "Just watch how much your drinking escalates when we take away your little potty-poo."

He was right about that, too. I already noticed I was drinking more than I used to. (I later learned that Neal should never have said those things to me. "The only requirement for membership is a desire to stop drinking," as the program says. But I'm glad Neal was brutally honest with me. He made me afraid I'd get kicked out if I didn't do what he said, and I'd never been pot-free for two weeks before).

That weekend I got together with some of the Purdue Pikes in Temecula, California—- a couple hours south of Ontario. Several of the Pikes lived in the area and Charlie and Anne were out visiting from Boston. I decided I wouldn't drink that weekend. I'd just see what happened. No drinking, no smoking.

"Not even a cocktail?" the always-delightful Anne asked.

"I'm just gonna try," I said. "I'll see how it goes."

"I think that's great," her happy-go-lucky husband Charlie said. "Good for you."

Of course, I was embarrassed that nobody tried to persuade me to go ahead and join them in taking a drink or smoking a joint. Our years of partying left a trail of my pictures in various drunken poses. There was plenty of photo evidence of my outrageous behavior.

I declared my first full day of sobriety to be that following Monday, August 20, 1990.

\* \* \*

Working as a substitute teacher is a thankless task. The regular teachers are required by their contract to leave lessons for the sub, but sometimes folks get sick in the middle of the night and can't make it to school. I learned a few survival tricks like carrying a deck of Trivial Pursuit cards and breaking the kids into competing teams. In English classes, I'd often put a prompt on the board and have the kids write about a subject like their goals for the future or a response to an inspirational statement.

Kids call it like they see it. My bulging eyes became the focus for many of the classes I taught. I'd often find drawings that were left on desks or the floor, after the bell rang. Sometimes the eyes were as big as the entire page and the caption "Teacher" was written across the top.

Other times students would speak as they left the room or when I passed them on the campus, "Hi, Miss Frog Eyes." Rather than be sensitive or feel hurt, I chose to hear their words as honest feedback. They were only describing what they saw.

I met with a surgeon at USC Medical Center who was an expert in eye problems related to Graves' disease. He explained that I could have surgery (orbital blepharoplasty) to correct my appearance, but the condition would still be present. I was also having other issues with my eyes. They were bulged out so far, they didn't close completely. I slept with extra pillows elevating my head, and I was going through mega-bottles of artificial tears because the eyes were always so dry. I could barely tolerate wearing my contact lenses, either.

"Graves' causes swelling behind the eyes and pushes them forward," the surgeon said. "One alternative to the surgery is to use a laser to push the eyes back in position. The only problem is there's a possibility of side effects."

"Like what?" I asked.

"Some people end up with double vision," he said.

"If I wanted double vision, I'd drink again," I told my friends. We scheduled my surgery.

# 17

# A Worker Among Workers

The morning of surgery my good buddy Meegan offered to drive me to the hospital. He was an actor friend I met at the Friday night alcoholic support group meetings at SAG headquarters. (Meegan helped escalate my growth. When I had six months clean and sober, he took me to my first meeting specifically for marijuana addicts. That program became a cornerstone of my sobriety because I related to people with a pot obsession.)

As the nurse prepped me for the eye operation, she took my vitals.

"Wow. Your blood pressure is 89 over 60," she said. "You do realize you're going in for major surgery, right?"

"Maybe I should be afraid, but I'm not," I said. "I trust the doctor."

"He's very good."

My genuine sense of well-being came from the spiritual faith of my recovery program and involvement with the Unitarian Universalist Church of Studio City. However, I needed to be awake for this medical adventure.

"We'll need you to blink during the procedure," he said. "The muscles need to stretch to cover the eyeball, but not sag."

As I lay on the table surrounded by the medical team, I felt the sting of the numbing injections, then the tug as they slit across each eyelid. A rush of warm blood poured into my scalp.

"Shit," I thought. "Maybe I should have been more nervous. This is a big fucking deal!"

After the surgery, I looked as if I'd been beaten. My eyes were both black and blue for weeks, but I bought huge Jackie Kennedy style dark glasses and continued to work as a sub every day. When students behaved like untamed animals, I threatened to show them the stitches on my eyes if they didn't straighten up. It worked. They feared the horrific sight.

I subbed for almost a year with LAUSD schools, declining several offers for full-time positions. One day, however, a no-nonsense vice principal, Virginia, at Fulton Middle School came into my room.

"Our special education classes are overcrowded so we're opening a new section. The teachers agree that you'd be a good fit for the position. What do you think?"

It sounded ideal. Special ed. students were dear to my heart. I always felt useful after subbing in those classes, because the kids had such an obvious need for help. The student/teacher ratio was also more manageable.

General ed. classes could have more than forty students per class (times five or six classes per day). Kids in San Fernando Valley general ed. classrooms could speak up to nine different languages, and some who came from abroad were in their first formal educational setting. I accepted several long-term sub jobs in various general ed. classes and felt overwhelmed, drained, and ineffective. After one particular social studies stint, I realized I'd been teaching a subject I didn't know in a language they didn't speak. It wasn't a fair situation for any of us.

With special education, kids had to meet certain criteria. Their academic performance had to be at least two years behind their actual age. Class size limits (at the time) were set for approximately fifteen students per teacher, with an adult aide. Granted, some of the kids struggled with severe behavior disorders, but I still thought my odds of success were better.

"It's the perfect gig," I said to Meegan. "There are few acting jobs every day, but tons of people who want them. Special ed. is a subject where there are way more openings than there are qualified teachers."

"I'll take it," I said to Virginia.

In December of 1991, on the cusp of my 42$^{nd}$ birthday, I signed my first contract to be a full-time teacher. Welcome, at last, to adulting.

* * *

After I'd been in LA for three years, Rena finally came to live with me. Gesualdo and Rosemary had provided her stable home and were getting married.

"I'm ready to move to California," she said.

I was thrilled and intimidated that I'd have my little girl back with me.

Kyrie enrolled at Indiana University, was living in a dorm with her high school best friend Jenny and continuing to date Travis. That is, until Travis went on a TV Lottery show where he won one million, fifteen thousand dollars. Several months later he broke up with Kyrie.

"You'll have a fabulous time studying in Spain," I told her.

"Yeh, I can't wait to take the summer classes and travel Europe when I finish," she said.

\* \* \*

As a teacher, I had the professional courtesy of school selection for my child.

"I want Rena at Van Nuys High School because it's right down the street from my school. If she has any trouble with her diabetes, I need to be able to get to her quickly," I told the smiling enrollment gal.

"Kids at Van Nuys will look very different from your Indiana school. There will be kids from a mix of nationalities," I said to Rena.

To make friends, she got involved in activities. During her sophomore year, she made the drill team, and immediately had a beautiful rainbow of girlfriends. She thrived on the LA experience. As a junior she became a varsity cheerleader, and I watched every football game.

"I'm not going to do cheerleading next year," Rena said at the end of that year.

"Your body will probably thank you," I said. Her diabetes created a delicate balance challenge between the rigorous exercise and her blood sugar levels.

"I think it's time you stopped going to family groups, concentrate on your sobriety and make living amends to your daughter," my alcoholic recovery mentor Shelley said.

In the performing arts magnet Rena performed in the spring musical all three years of high school. Mother and Dad drove across the country to see all her shows, too. I was grateful I could support Rena in all these endeavors.

As she neared graduation, Rena decided to return to the Midwest for college.

"Who knows how long my grandparents will be alive," she said."I don't want to be away from all of them for another four years."

"She's been accepted at Purdue!" I told Gesualdo when the admission letter arrived.

"That's wonderful," he said. "I'm glad she'll be back in Indiana where I can see her more often."

In the meantime, Kyrie received a gut punch when she returned from her study abroad.

"Travis dated Jenny while I was in Spain," Kyrie said on the phone. She and Jenny were cheerleaders together in middle and high school before they were college roommates. "They just announced they're getting married."

The two people Kyrie loved and trusted most—- who both spoke badly about the other during the four years Kyrie and Travis dated—- were now engaged.

As her college graduation drew near, Kyrie called.

"How much did it cost for you and Dad to make your first demo tape?" she asked.

"A few hundred dollars, why?"

"I've decided I'm too young to just go straight to work after I graduate. I want to move to LA and become a singer."

"That's fantastic!" I said, though the idea alarmed me.

Though years of weekly phone calls brought Kyrie and me closer, tension lingered between us whenever we were physically together.

"She's never forgiven me ruining our family when I brought Landon into our lives," I told my sponsor, Shelley. "I'm not sure Kyrie and I can live peacefully under one roof."

After graduation from I.U., she packed up and moved in with Rena and me. Rena was leaving for Purdue at the end of the summer, so Kyrie agreed to drive across the country with her sister and fly back.

Once the two girls left town, I decided to force Kyrie out on her own. We were already sniping at each other, and I no longer felt comfortable in my own home. I could foresee a murder/suicide in the offing, and I wasn't sure which of us would be the perpetrator.

"Just do it," my sober sister, Sue said.

I called Kyrie at her dad's. "When you get back to LA you'll need to find a place to live," I said. "I'm moving to a one-bedroom place."

* * *

After Rena graduated, LAUSD made a change in school configurations.

"We'll be sending our ninth graders to the high school and need some of the staff to follow along," the principal said at our spring staff meeting.

Trading the oldest students for more childish sixth graders sounded like a brand of torture I couldn't endure.

"Put me on the list to follow the ninth graders," I said.

Just as Rena left, I joined the faculty of Van Nuys High School. I continued as a special day class English teacher in the new setting and was thrilled to be among the more mature and communicative high school population with their own special brand of hormonal crazy. Just as I had done at the middle school,

I became involved with the drug and alcohol Impact program for students who were self- or teacher- referred. I remained in that job for ten years, but left after a traumatic, tragic series of events.

# 18

# The end and the beginning

As I approached my classroom on May 2, 2005 two of my students walked toward me, sobbing.

"Eric is dead," Yvonne said through tears. "He was killed in a drive-by shooting."

Eric was a big, funny kid with a broad smile, and a sweet nature, but his neighborhood carried the tagged evidence of active gangsters. Maybe he was one, too. The incident leveled me. A student who I taught to read had been gunned down.

Within the week I had a run-in with another student, Monica. I will skip the details of the false accusation of abuse her conservator filed against me in 2005 and my yearlong battle to defend myself. I prefer to fast-forward to February 8, 2021 when I received this message on Facebook:

"Good morning Joyce. I don't know if you remember me but I was in your class 2003(-2005). I just want to tell you thank you for your hard work and I know I give (sic) you a rough time but now that I'm older I understand education was very important. And I just wanted to tell you that you were amazing Teacher."

When I met Monica, she, too couldn't read a word. This

imperfect message filled me with pride and relief sixteen years after one of my life's greatest horrors.

At the end of 2005 I left that job and spent eight years working in a job with special education seniors called Transition Services. The job was helping kids with disabilities determine what to do after high school and included many different transition activities. Sometimes I'd teach a lesson on how to read a pay stub or how to make change as a cashier. Other times I'd assist a student in getting their first job or finding a program to attend after graduation.

* * *

"Sorry Joyce, but I'm having health problems and the doctor says I need to cut back on my activity." It was my sponsor, Shelley. "I'm sure you will have no trouble finding a new sponsor. I love you and wish you a wonderful sober future."

I was seven years sober and loved Shelley. She was the person who directed me to stop identifying as "Joyce, alcoholic-pothead" in meetings.

"Feel free to be a pothead at marijuana recovery meetings, but just identify as a drunk in alcoholic groups to honor the 'singleness of purpose' idea."

Shelley also drilled into me the concept of self-responsibility, rather than blame.

"Where did you set the ball rolling?" she said every time I came whining about things or people that were bothering me.

My alcoholic recovery "home group" is like a small city within the large metropolitan LA community. People get together on weekends to celebrate birthdays for five-year increments of sobriety. When members get married or are expecting a child, we have bridal and baby showers. Group activities are designed for people to learn how to socialize without booze. I joined this group in June of 1997.

"I'm looking for a mentor in a successful heterosexual relationship," I asked a random trio of men.

They pointed me toward Judy G.

"You must commit to the Wednesday meeting, no matter what. If you ever have a conflict, you bring it to me, and I decide. If you accept that, I'm happy to work with you," she said.

She directed me to go to all the parties on the weekends.

"That's where you get to know people better and the group gets smaller to you."

At the first baby shower I attended there was a guy moving furniture around. I grabbed the opposite end of the couch he was carrying.

"I'm Paul," he said after we sat down.

"He's kinda cute," I thought.

From then on, I watched for Paul. I re-introduced myself the next time I saw him.

"How's school?" I asked. He was getting an MBA and working full time as a production manager at an industrial manufacturing company. He was twelve years younger than I, but with his gray hair, didn't seem too young to pursue.

In December he approached me at the meeting.

"Is that your name on the list for the New Year's show?" he asked.

"Yes."

"My roommate's in that show," he said.

"My mentor said I have to do it."

I was miffed about the whole thing. I'd been given a spot in the chorus—- no speaking lines. Talk about humbling....

"You don't know what a privilege it is just to be in the show!" Judy said.

When I got to the first rehearsal, I was shocked to see Paul there. Over the course of the next weeks, I got to know him better.

"I swear he's flirting with me, Diana" I said to my pal. "But he never asks for my number, and we live close to each other, but he never offers to carpool even though the rehearsals are on the other side of the hill." Paul and I lived in the San Fernando Valley, but rehearsals were in Culver City.

The night of the show he never left my side. We ate dinner together and danced every dance. At the end of the evening, he STILL hadn't asked for my number.

"The guy is a freak," I told my friends.

We're signing up for internet dating on January first," Diana said. "You interested?"

"I'm in!"

I'd spent most of my sobriety not dating. It took several years and three eye surgeries to get my appearance back to almost pre-Graves'. My few attempts at dating hadn't gone particularly well, either.

I was now eight years sober, and while people recommend not dating at the beginning of sobriety, I was impatient to meet a partner, damn it.

I loved the internet dating process.

"I'm not giving my number to anyone before we've had six email exchanges," I told Diana.

Just about this time Paul asked me out. For a split second I wanted to do both—- date him and continue the internet search. I'd begun emailing some of the guys but hadn't given my number to anyone (and had been rejected by every guy whose photo I selected).

"You've been wanting to date this guy for six months", I told myself."Just date his ass! If it doesn't work out, you can always go back to the internet."

It turns out Paul's most powerful role models for successful relationships were May/December combinations like ours.

"My grandmother's second husband was almost twenty years younger, and my mother's last fifteen-year relationship was also with a younger man," he said.

Paul and I have now been married twenty-four years. He is sober thirty-five years and I turned thirty-three years last August. Our lives center around maintaining our sobriety. We go to several meetings every week; both have individual mentors and attend meetings for alcoholics in recovery wherever we travel in the world.

* * *

Nine months after our marriage, Mother was diagnosed with tongue cancer. Six months later, Dad had a massive heart attack and lost oxygen to his brain for several minutes. They were living in Indiana in the tri-level house where we lived during my Junior High and High School years. Their primary caregiver was my sister Pam who'd had a heart attack at age forty-four.

My brother Gary and his wife JoAnn had moved to LA where he was now a vice-president at Warner Bros. Records and lived just a few minutes from Paul and me.

"We need to get Mother and Dad out here," I told him.

Pam put together a yard sale for Dad's collection of power

tools and Gary went back to help. I went to Indiana during my summer school break and spent three weeks packing up everything Mom and Dad owned.

Gesualdo, his wife Rosemary, all my former in-laws- everybody generously helped.

Mother and Dad lived in their house for thirty-seven years, so it was a gigantic job. While I was there, Gesualdo's gentle giant father, Earl, had a heart attack and died. Kyrie and Rena flew home for the funeral and were able to help me with the work at my parents' house.

\* \* \*

"After all the chemotherapy and radiation, do we know if mom still has cancer?" I asked the doctor.

"Every square inch of her mouth, throat and tongue are burnt from the radio-active isotopes they planted in her tongue. They pulsed radiation into the cancer, and it worked, but these are the side effects. They may have used excessive amounts." the doctor at IU Medical Center said.

Mother was in extreme pain, and on heavy-duty opioid medication. Despite it all, she sat in the living room, dabbing at her drooling mouth as she recalled where, in their world travels, all the fascinating things came from.

"Tell us more stories," former sister-in-law Cindy said as she held up a letter written from my dad on their honeymoon over fifty years earlier.

"We got all the pendulum clocks in Germany, Dad bought the Noritake China in Viet Nam, I brought the tea set home from Japan," she said.

We found the receipt from their honeymoon night where Dad spent a whopping $4 for the room. It was a poignant, unforgettable experience watching mom look at all her treasures as we wrapped and boxed them carefully, uncertain of her current health condition.

Mother was on a g-tube, unable to eat, for three years. Just months before my father passed from a final heart attack, she had grueling surgery to remove a radiation-infected jawbone, replace it with bone from her leg and a skin graft from her thigh.

"Because your mother is diabetic," the doctor said, "She'll require hyperbaric oxygenation to heal from the surgery."

I'd heard Michael Jackson owned one of those chambers and used it to retain his youthful appearance.

"Is there room for me to squeeze in next to her?" I asked the doctor.

After several months of treatments, mom's incisions were repaired, and she required only Tylenol for pain management. I began writing this book while waiting the hours for each healing session to end.

* * *

Paul and I moved Mom and Dad from Indianapolis to Los Angeles in August of 2001. They bought a condo in the same building where we live. For Dad's final two years of life, I had the nightly honor of preparing his dinner since mom was still on a g-tube.

In April 2002, my phone rang.

"Joyce, this is Micheal. I'm at Community Hospital. Your sister had a massive heart attack, and it doesn't look good."

"Oh my God! What happened?"

"They've been working on her for several hours, but they told me nothing's working and her organs are starting to fail. I think you folks better get back here."

Gary and I scooped our parents up and flew them back to Indy. Pam was unrecognizable when we entered her room. She was in a coma, her chest was covered with a drape, but it was open from the failed attempts to get her heart to work. Each of us and her thirty-seven-year-old daughter, Beth, said goodbye to her.

"Please disconnect the machines," Mother told the doctor.

* * *

"Who's in that casket?" Dad asked as we sat in the cemetery waiting for the small group of friends and family to arrive.

"It's Pam, Dad," I said.

"You're kidding me!"

Again, Gesualdo, Rosemary and Cindy swept in to help me hold a quick yard sale, find a home for Pam's dog, and get her daughter Beth moved in with her father.

Several months later, we learned Pam had a life insurance policy for Beth who has multiple disabilities and requires supervision to manage her medication and healthcare. The insurance allowed us to hire an attorney, set up a special needs trust, and move Beth to LA where she requested to live. I've been her conservator the past twenty-two years and today she lives in a wonderful group home, goes to a work training day-program, and joins us for family events and outings.

When Mother turned 80 our entire family, including my kids, their partners, Gesualdo, Rosemary and Beth all traveled to Hawaii where Gary and I hosted her birthday party on Oahu in

December 2007.

The banquet room at Scofield Barracks Army Base was filled with mother's immediate and distant family and friends decked out in their best Aloha shirts and Muumuus. My daughters and I surprised her with a hula, as did her eldest sister, Jane, and several other cousins. Gesualdo delighted her with a song he wrote for her.

"Everyone should have a party like that before they die," mom told us when we returned to L.A.

\* \* \*

Just one year later, Paul and I traveled with the girls and their men to Syracuse, New York for the annual air guitar party with our Purdue Pike crew. The party is a tradition requiring folks to travel to that year's host city prepared to compete for the coveted traveling trophy. We bring costumes, props and anything that can serve as a fake guitar. The parties began in 1973 and continue to this day. In 2008 we assembled in Syracuse where the frigid temperatures failed to interrupt the warm feasts and festivities hosts Dave and Peg supplied.

Gary had retired, he and his wife, JoAnn now lived back in Indy, and had just returned home after spending Christmas with mom and us in L.A.

"Your mom keeps falling, but she won't let us take her to the hospital," the voice on the phone said. The staff from mom's assisted-living apartment were looking after her.

"Let me speak with her " I said. "Mother, please don't give these folks a hard time. Let them call an ambulance."

Alas, there was a snowstorm in Syracuse and all flights were delayed. My treasured friend, Barbara, in L.A. went to check on Mother and arrived while I was on the phone with her explaining our snowbound dilemma.

"We'll be there as soon as possible, mom. Do you want me to have Gary come back?"

"Yes," mom said. "I can't do ANYTHING. I can't even hold the phone."

"Then hand the phone to Barbara," I said. "We all love you and will get there as quickly as we can."

Those were the last words Mother ever spoke to me. By the time we arrived, she was paralyzed from the neck down and was intubated.

"She has Guillain-Barré Syndrome," the doctor said. "Her age and diabetes make it difficult to recover."

We all spent as much time as possible with her, but Mother was gone in just two months. During those months she could only shake her head and blink her eyes. We tried to hold her hands, put lotion on her feet, anything to comfort her. One day Gary arrived at the hospital and raced to mom's side.

"Hey Mom, when we rub your hands and feet does it feel like needles poking into you?"

Her eyes got wide, and she mouthed the word "YES!" as she shook her head up and down.

"I just read that Guillain-Barré causes neuropathy," Gary said. "Mom, I'm so sorry we've been torturing you!"

We brought a CD player and asked staff to please keep her favorite music playing, so she was surrounded with the Josh Groban, Nora Jones and The Judds tunes, among others. One day the girls' guys brought ukuleles and we all surrounded the hospital bed to sing another batch of her faves. For Valentine's Day Gary and Paul sent the Sweet Adeline's a Capella singers to serenade her. My cousin Joey and his wife also came to sing classic Hawaiian tunes. I like to think we sang my Mother to sleep. She died on February 27, 2008.

\* \* \*

On March 9 Pickwick Gardens in Burbank was alive with nature's colors and fragrance, the skies were azure, and goodie bags were waiting for guests in the reception room.

"You're making fun of Mom. That's a terrible idea," Gary said.

"Well, regardless of my lack of qualifications, I'm the matriarch of the family now and I think it's a sweet tribute to her," I said.

Everyone received a small baggie containing a package of tissues, a handwritten cookie recipe card and a four-leaf clover Mother handpicked from her Indiana yard. I'm not saying the lady had too much time on her hands, but she self-laminated each green good-luck token with transparent tape. To this day I still have a baggie full of her handiwork. Mother loved to protect things by keeping them in baggies...sometimes baggies inside of baggies. As we went through her clothing, we found tissues in every pocket of every garment and her delicious cookie baking tradition lives on every holiday season.

"The kids got me the final video, but I haven't had time to watch it," Kyrie said. A year prior she hired former students to videotape her interviewing mother. The young videographers captured mom's memories for all of us.

It was surreal to sit at her memorial watching the short footage of mom speaking to her mourners. Two of her sisters,

Alice and Annie, attended and the senior living director brought a vanload of friends from there, too. Gary's work friends and my recovery family packed the room. When it came to the moment Kyrie asked on the film, "Tell me about my mom," Mother dabbed at her mouth then said without hesitation, "She was a live wire from the time she was born. She is the most wonderful daughter. She's so sweet."

How do you go from being the kid about whom her mom said, "I wish I'd had dogs instead of children," to the person she described at the end of her days?

My personal transformation, my evolution, was through the endless hours of alcoholic and family recovery meetings. I go to meetings almost every day. I have a sponsor, continue studying and working the twelve steps and I sponsor others in recovery. There's no explaining why that works, but it has worked for me to "practice the principles of the program in all of my affairs" for 33 years. I've adopted the philosophy attributed to Eric Clapton when he said, "I play guitar between meetings." If I tell myself whatever I'm doing is something I'm doing between meetings, it loses its urgency. Whether or not I book that acting job, the political winds blow my way or folks finally put down their stupid guns, I'm busy trying to be my best self...between meetings. Even when I come up short, act like a jackass in traffic, wish bad things for insurrectionists, it's just the thing I do between meetings. One day at a time.

I continue to pursue acting. In 2023 I was honored to portray Anne Smith, one of the founders of the family recovery program, Al-Anon, in a 17-week run at Theatre 68 in North Hollywood. The play Bill W. & Dr. Bob tells the story of the founding of Alcoholics Anonymous. It was the magical merging of two of my lifelong passions...recovery and performing.

I lose a friend, relative, or personally favorite icon almost every month these days. Life is fleeting. When it's my time, I honestly believe I will be able to rest in peace.

Thanks for letting me share.

# Epilogue

My brother Gary and his wife JoAnn moved back to the Midwest when they retired twenty years ago. We get together when we can, depending on their availability. They are central to the caregiving team for JoAnn's parents who are both in their nineties.

Gesualdo and Rosemary have been married for over thirty years. We see them whenever they come to LA to visit our daughter, Kyrie, and granddaughter. We also get together at the annual Air Guitar competitions/reunions with our Purdue Pike friends. In 2022 we collaborated on an act and won the trophy for our Doors' "People are Strange" performance conceived by Rosemary.

I'm still in touch with Landon's family. He's been married to a wonderful gal for over twenty years, is retired and loves to spend his mornings as his father did...sitting on the porch drinking coffee and smoking cigarettes. We wish each other well. His parents split when he and I were together and I wrote this song, "Pretty Baby Blues," about my view of the dynamics of their divorce. The last line kind of sums up my life, too.

Pretty Baby, I had enough
I couldn't take it livin' offfa the cuff
You didn't think that I could reply

With a fistful of anger wavin' good-bye
You been pushin' me hard
And it was getting' me down
You took advantage you know
This is the end, babe, and I gotta go
But wake up- a break up is all that it's been
Won't stop you, I'll drop you
Let someone else in
Saw you with a girl by your side
You were leavin'- tryin' to hide
I'm fed up now with alla your stuff
I'm tellin' you now, I just had enough
I was lookin' around
There's a man that I found
There's a new game and new rules
I can't believe I was a fool
But see here, I'm free here
I'm movin' along
I want you, I'll haunt you
I'm travelin' on
Pretty Baby lives with another
He knows our baby's a mother
Saw each other cruisin' last Sunday
He couldn't find the time for a wave
So long since I held Pretty Baby
I remember the years that we had
I will take my love for him to the grave of my coffin
Wish him well as we go on our own
But hush up- a bust up
Is all that it's been
We had love, we have love

## We traveled along

# Afterword

aviva.grandprints@gmail.com

# About the Author

Joyce Fidler is a first time writer whose previous compositions included songs for her 80s new wave bands. Her foray into writing comes after a busy life as co-owner of a record store/-headshop, singer with a video on MTV (to a song she wrote), university communications instructor, secondary special educator, and actor. She wrote a one-woman show, *Evolution of a Pisces Baby Boomer* which she staged 5 times at 3 LA theatres prior to the Covid pandemic.

An Army brat who's lived in Germany, Japan and around the U.S., Joyce and her hot husband live in Los Angeles where they will soon celebrate 25 years of marriage- a personal best. Her grown daughters (who both survived her lousy parenting) are thriving in LA and Australia with their beautiful families. Joyce has a BA from Purdue in Speech Education and Theatre, a MS in Radio-Television from Butler and Special Education credential from Cal State Northridge.

**You can connect with me on:**

- 🌐 https://joycefidler.com
- 🅵 https://www.facebook.com
- 🔗 https://www.instagram.com/enerjoyce
- 🔗 https://www.threads.net/@enerjoyce
- 🔗 https://www.tiktok.com/en

www.ingramcontent.com/pod-product-compliance
Lightning Source LLC
LaVergne TN
LVHW041322080426
835513LV00008B/557